MEMPHIS

IN BLACK AND WHITE

Old and new conveyances mingled with pedestrians during rush hour in downtown Memphis.

THE
MAKING OF AMERICA
SERIES

MEMPHIS
IN BLACK AND WHITE

BEVERLY G. BOND AND
JANANN SHERMAN

ARCADIA

Published by Arcadia Publishing
an imprint of Tempus Publishing Inc.
Charleston SC, Chicago, Portsmouth NH, San Francisco

For all general information contact Arcadia Publishing at:
Telephone 843-853-2070
Fax 843-853-0044
E-Mail sales@arcadiapublishing.com
For customer service and orders:
Toll-Free 1-888-313-2665

Visit us on the Internet at http://www.arcadiapublishing.com

CONTENTS

ACKNOWLEDGMENTS

Special thanks to the following individuals and institutions for their invaluable assistance in helping us locate information and images of this unforgettable city: Jim Johnson, Patricia LaPointe, and Greg Newby in the History Department of the Memphis/Shelby County Library and Information Center; Ed Frank and Jim Cole of Special Collections at the University of Memphis Libraries; and John Dougan, Shelby County Archivist; Harley Melton, our research assistant; and Charles Sherman and Geraldus Bond who provided the mental space and encouragement to write about a city we all love.

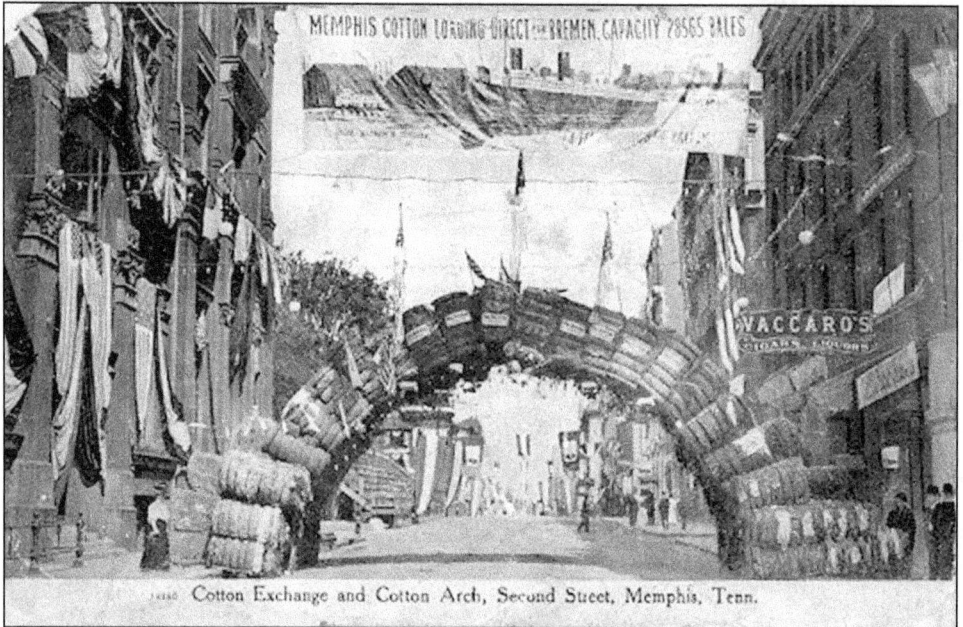

Cotton Exchange and Cotton Arch, Second Street, Memphis, Tenn.

During the season, cotton bales were piled high along Memphis streets. This arch of cotton bales, constructed in 1907, reaches across Second Street near the Cotton Exchange. The shipping banner over the street reads, "Memphis Cotton Loading Direct for Bremen, Capacity 28,565 Bales."

INTRODUCTION

Memphis is a city in black and white, a vibrant city with a divided heart. It is a city of contrasts and contradictions where southern charm and elegance meet southern tension and violence. For much of its history, Memphis has been inhabited by and divided by two peoples who share a common place and history but are separated by the social and political differences ascribed to race.

Memphis is the capital city of the Mississippi Delta; a land of rich soil and grinding poverty. Defined and dominated by the ceaseless and unpredictable Mississippi River, the city's strategic location made it a natural distribution port and center of commerce. Settlers to the rich agricultural hinterlands around the city brought cotton culture and slave labor to the mid-South. As the gateway to the lower South and the trans-Mississippi West, Memphis became the largest inland cotton market in the world. Later development of roads, railroads, and air service sustained the city's dominance in transportation and distribution, a position reinforced in the late twentieth century by Federal Express. Memphis International Airport handles more air cargo than any other field in the world.

Memphis is a city that is progressive and provincial at the same time, a volatile mix of rich and poor, black and white, rural and urban, old and new. African Americans, once freed of legal bondage, came to the city seeking a better life. Ironically, their greatest cultural legacy—Memphis music—is a product of the misery they fled and the poverty and divisiveness they found.

As the twenty-first century begins, there are hopeful signs of the old bifurcated system breaking down. This is the result of Herculean efforts of blacks and whites to bridge the racial divide as well as the influx of other groups who have complicated the simple binary of black and white. The newest migrants to Memphis include an estimated half-million Latinos, Asians, Africans, and people from the Middle East. Cultural awareness festivals dot the social calendar; the largest of them all is the month-long Memphis in May celebration. The month begins and ends with a celebration of music: the three-day Beale Street Music Festival showcases Memphis' reputation as the Home of the Blues and the Birthplace of Rock 'n' Roll. It ends with the Sunset Symphony and Memphis family picnic on the banks of the Mississippi River. In between, we celebrate

Memphis' most famous export, barbecue, with the World Championship Barbecue Contest.

Memphis remains endlessly fascinating and complex, a city that still draws people with its music, its vitality, its promise.

Artist Charles Graham sketched the Memphis levee in 1887.

1. AT THE FOURTH BLUFF

From a strategic location high above the Mississippi River at the Fourth Bluff between Cairo, Illinois, and New Orleans, Louisiana, Memphis has been a center for transit, trade, and commerce for most of its history. Indian and European nations recognized the importance of the site and contested for power in the region long before American settlers arrived. Native Americans inhabited the region about 10,000 years ago. Over the next 9,000 years, Native-American groups moved gradually through the Archaic and Woodland stages, and in the Mississippian stage (800 A.D.) cities and primitive city-states emerged.

The most famous of these cities and city-states was Cahokia, across from the present-day site of St. Louis. Yet remains of Mississippian culture in western Tennessee have been found at Pinson Mound, 80 miles east of present-day Memphis, and at Chisca's Mound and Chucalissa in Shelby County. These sites were part of a string of towns along the Mississippi River south of present-day Memphis. Mississippian culture was characterized by trade and a growing reliance on corn cultivation, sizable concentrations of populations, social stratification, hereditary chiefdoms, and the construction of large flat-top mounds. These mounds were used as platforms for temples and as the living quarters for chiefs and priests.

The town of Chucalissa (Choo-kah-le-sah) was established around 1000 A.D. but was abandoned and resettled over the next 500 years. About 1500, Chucalissa's residents constructed large mounds, houses, and storage facilities around a central plaza where social and economic interaction took place. Archaeological excavations at Chucalissa, begun in the 1940s and 1950s, unearthed a Temple Mound where the Chief's House was constructed, as well as dwelling sites, burial mounds, skeletal remains, pottery, and artifacts. The Chief's House, a 50-square-foot structure built in the center of the mound, contained a large central hearth used for food preparation and subterranean storage pits where food and household utensils were stored. The floor was made of fired clay. Other houses in the village averaged 15 to 20 square feet. A mixture of mud and grass was used to cover the walls and native grasses to thatch the roof. In the 1500s, Chucalissa's residents hunted bear, deer, turkey, and small game with bows and arrows or fished the Mississippi River or its tributaries for gar, carp, drum, or turtle. An artisan class made up of potters, weavers, and shaman enriched the cultural life of the community. Chucalissa's residents also traded surplus goods with neighboring villages.

Spain claimed much of the southern part of North America but did little to establish permanent settlements until the middle of the sixteenth century. In 1542, when Hernando De Soto arrived in what would eventually become Tennessee, he had already been in North America for three years. He had served as a captain in Francisco Pizarro's forces when the latter attacked the Incas of Peru in the 1530s. In 1539, in command of his own 600-man army, De Soto landed at Tampa Bay in Florida. He and his army marched through the Southeast before arriving in present-day Tennessee in 1540. Their relationships with Indians in the area were probably peaceful until they demanded food, information, and women from a group of Chiscas living near the upper Nolichuky River.

De Soto and his men were searching for gold and silver to rival what had been discovered by other Spanish conquistadors. Attracted by tales of prosperous native villages in the Mississippi River valley, De Soto's army arrived in the area of the Chickasaw Bluffs in 1542. They spent several weeks building rafts before crossing the river in early June at a point south of present-day Memphis and advancing north and west through Arkansas. After a winter of exploration and plunder, De Soto and his men began their return journey, probably along the Arkansas or the Red Rivers, down to the Mississippi. They occupied an Indian village called Guachoya where De Soto became ill and died on May 21, 1542. His body was weighed down with sand and thrown into the Mississippi River. The Native Americans were told that he had ascended into heaven.

In the two centuries following De Soto's visit, Indian cultures in the region of the Fourth Bluff declined in the face of disease and internal conflict. Spanish explorers brought smallpox, influenza, and measles for which the Indians had no natural immunity. The Spanish also attacked and ravaged native communities searching for gold and capturing slaves. Surviving communities relocated, split into smaller units, or formed confederacies like the northeastern Iroquois Confederation or the southeastern Five Civilized Tribes.

By the eighteenth century, the Chickasaws were the dominant tribe in the Mississippi Valley, but they faced a new set of European adventurers as France staked her claim to the region. French fur trappers, traders, and missionaries traveled from the valley of the St. Lawrence River through the Mississippi River Basin. In 1673, Father Jacques Marquette and fur trapper Louis Joliet traveled down the Mississippi River in a small canoe as far as the mouth of the Arkansas River in search of a route to the Pacific Ocean. They stopped at the Monsoupeleas or Mosopeleas Village of Agenatchi at one of the bluffs. Marquette wrote in his journal that the Indians "wear their hair long and mark their bodies in the Iroquois fashion; the head-dress and clothing of their women were like those of Huron squaws."[1] Marquette described houses constructed by inhabitants on a system of elevated wooden grids. Underneath these grids they would place smudge pots and over them they hung animal pelts to combat the mosquitoes.

Flat-top mounds similar to the De Soto Mound just south of the old Frisco Bridge were an important aspect of the Mississippian culture of the Woodland Indians.

The Indians served the two explorers a meal of buffalo meat and bears' oil with plums; but it was clear that the Frenchmen were not the first Europeans in the region since the Native Americans possessed guns, axes, hoes, knives, beads, and double-glass bottles.

Nine years after Marquette and Joliet visited Agenatchi, Robert Cavalier de La Salle passed by the Fourth Bluff on his journey to New Orleans. His journey was part of a French strategy to counter English and Spanish influence in North America by establishing a string of trading posts from the headwaters of the Mississippi River to the Gulf of Mexico. La Salle led a group of 54 Frenchmen and Indians to the area near the Chickasaw Bluffs. One of his men, Pierre Prudhomme, disappeared while hunting and La Salle constructed a small fort, Fort Prudhomme, as a temporary base while the group searched for the man. Prudhomme returned two days later and La Salle and his men continued their journey south. But before he left the region, La Salle named a small river near the Fourth Bluff after a Loup Indian, Mayot, who accompanied his party. Riviere a Mayot became the Riviere du Loup; the name was eventually translated to the Wolf River. La Salle's brother, Abbe Jean Cavalier, wrote the first description of what he called the "Chickasaw Bluffs." He described them as "precipices rising to a height of eighty to a hundred feet; all of different colored earths" and extending for a "league and a half" (about 4.5 miles) on the right side of the river.[2]

Pottery bowls were recovered in archaeological excavations at Chucalissa Indian village near T.O. Fuller State Park. Chucalissa was established, abandoned, and resettled several times between 1000 and the 1500s.

As in other parts of North America, relationships between the French and Native Americans along the Mississippi River were relatively peaceful. France's agricultural settlements were clustered along the St. Lawrence River and, unlike English, Dutch, and other foreign colonists, the French *coureurs de bois* (runners of the woods) were more concerned with trade than with permanent settlement. They needed the Indians to help supply a growing European market for furs. However, conflicts in Europe from the late seventeenth century through the middle of the eighteenth century had serious implications for all European colonists and Indians.

From 1688 until 1763, European nations were involved in a series of wars for world domination. Most of the fighting occurred in Europe, but some conflicts spilled over to European colonies throughout the world, including North America. English and French armies and their respective Indian allies battled in the Native American territory between New England and New France.

In the Treaty of Utrecht, which ended the third war (the War of the Spanish Succession or Queen Anne's War), Louis XIV placed his grandson on the Spanish throne as King Philip V of Spain, but the Spanish and French thrones were to remain permanently separate. More important for colonial North America, some French territory in Canada, including Arcadia (renamed Nova Scotia), was ceded to the British.

Despite the territorial losses, France tried, with little success, to strengthen her colonial presence by reinforcing the forts in the Mississippi Valley. In 1729, a group of Natchez Indians massacred a French garrison at Fort Rosalie in retaliation for brutal treatment of the Indians by the French. The French responded by nearly wiping out the Natchez Indians. The few survivors conveyed their intense hatred for the French to the Chickasaw bands they joined, and this enmity soon affected life in the region. Seven years after the Fort Rosalie massacre, when Jean Baptiste Le Moyne, Sieur de Bienville, traveled up the Tombignee River from New Orleans to join another French army coming down river, the Chickasaws defeated each army before they could unite. In 1739, Bienville again tried to reassert French control over the region by constructing Fort Assumption at the Fourth Bluff as a base from which his 3,500-man army of Frenchmen and Indians could lead attacks on neighboring Chickasaw towns. But Bienville's army, weakened by disease and desertion, was forced to abandon the fort and return to New Orleans.

Like much of the American continent, the Fourth Bluff was caught up in the global tussles between England, France, and Spain for power. The struggle in the American colonies came to a head with the French and Indian War (1754–1763). Unlike the three preceding conflicts, the French and Indian War began with clashes between French troops and militia from Virginia in the Ohio Valley and spread to the European continent. In the aftermath of this war, a victorious England claimed

Jean Baptiste Le Moyne, Sieur de Bienville, acted as civil and military governor of Louisiana.

all French territories east of the Mississippi River, but control of the river and France's western territories went to Spain. Britain now faced the problem of governing her far-flung empire with a depleted treasury. The continuing discord between settlers and Indians were among Britain's most pressing problems in the Americas. The Proclamation of 1763, which prohibited migration west of the Appalachian Mountains, was designed to make it easier for Britain to manage relations in the new western territories, but to Americans who had fought to wrest these territories from the French, England's actions seemed repressive and tyrannical. Besides, it was a proclamation impossible to enforce. Britain's armies were spread thinly throughout America's coastal settlements, leaving colonists free to move around in the territories west of the Proclamation Line.

Dumont's map shows the lands of the Chickasaw and Choctaw Indians and the location of Fort Assumption.

2. THREE FLAGS
AT THE FOURTH BLUFF

In 1763, the Chickasaws controlled the Fourth Bluff, but they used the area primarily as hunting grounds and as a trading site. Weakened by warfare with the French and by exposure to Old World diseases, they hoped for peaceful relationships with the British. The English had little time or money to spend on Indian problems in the west. Despite the terms of the Proclamation of 1763, American migration west of the Appalachian Mountains went virtually unchecked in the three decades following the ouster of the French and the transfer of their Louisiana territory to British and Spanish control. The Spanish established the northern boundary of their territory on the east bank of the Mississippi River at the Yazoo River and conceded the territory north of this point to the British. In 1766, Englishman Thomas Hutchins visited the Fourth Bluff and noted its prospects as a "commanding, airy, pleasant, and extensive situation for settlements."[3] Hutchins was probably the first European to think of the Fourth Bluff as a site for a permanent town.

During the Revolutionary War, although officially loyal to their British allies, the Chickasaws were also allied with individual American rebels such as James Robertson of Nashville. Americans negotiated for the right to construct forts in Chickasaw territory, and the tribe focused their anger on the Spanish who controlled the Mississippi River and the Louisiana Territory. From their sanctuary on the Wolf River, Chickasaw raiding parties, led by James Logan Colbert, the Scotsman who was their chief, attacked Spanish vessels. Colbert was married to three Chickasaw sisters and his sons William (Chooshemataha), George (Tootmastubbe), Levi (Itawamba), and James (no Indian name is recorded for this fourth son), were prominent figures in relations between the tribe and Americans in the nineteenth century.

When the Revolutionary War ended, the Chickasaws transferred their political allegiance from Britain to the new American nation, but relations at the Fourth Bluff remained unsettled into the next decade. The Fourth Bluff was the focus of a three-way power struggle between the Chickasaws, the Americans, and the Spanish. As American farmers moved into the Old Southwest, the Mississippi

River was an increasingly important transportation artery for Midwestern and mid-Southern farmers and traders. Spanish control of the river restricted the ability of American farmers to fully exploit the region. National leaders continually renegotiated with Spain for the right to navigate the Mississippi, but not to the satisfaction of either nation. Like the French before them, American settlers decided to construct a fort at the Fourth Bluff to limit Spanish influence. The fort would also encourage trade through Nashville rather than the Spanish cities of Pensacola and Mobile. But the Spanish decided to resolve the conflict by declaring the Chickasaw nation a Spanish dependency and constructing fortifications at the Fourth Bluff from which they could govern the region.

In 1795, the Spanish sent Dom Manuel Gayoso de Lemos, governor of the Natchez district, to purchase land from the Chickasaws and establish a garrison at the Wolf and Mississippi Rivers. Gayoso, with the assistance of Benjamin Fooy, a Dutch immigrant who had lived within the tribe in the 1780s, negotiated with pro-Spanish Chickasaw leader Ugulayacabe for the site. Gayoso brought in artillery and raised the Spanish flag at Fort San Fernando de las Barrancas, or St. Ferdinand of the Bluffs, on May 30, 1795. He considered the fort an extension of his river fleet of three barges (*La Felipa*, *La Flecha*, and *El Rayo*) that were anchored nearby.

Bounded by Bayou Gayoso, the Wolf River, the Mississippi River, and Nonconnah Creek, the fort was situated on a point that was militarily

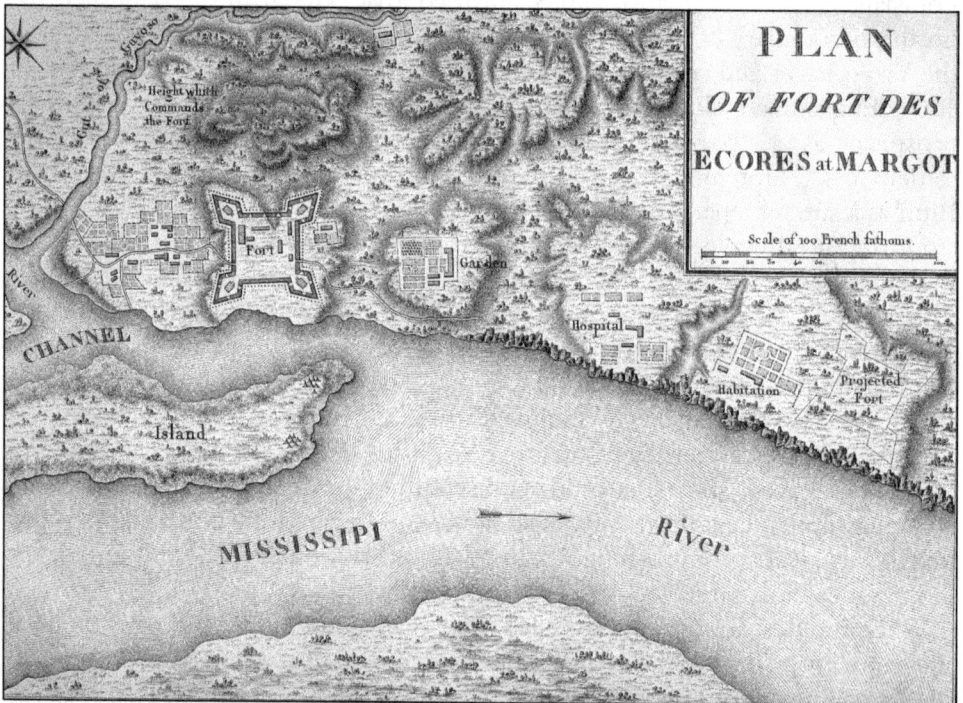

Fort San Fernando, established in 1795 by Don Manuel Gayoso de Lemos, was named in honor of Ferdinand VII of Spain.

indefensible. It was at the first high ground beyond Bayou Gayoso, but was surrounded on the east and south by higher ground that might be occupied by an enemy force. The view upriver was also obstructed by an island at the mouth of the Wolf River. Garrisoned by a force of over 125 men and with eight 8-pounders as artillery, Fort San Fernando had a central square that was 200 feet on each side, with diagonal bastions extending another 75 feet at each corner. The commander's residence, barracks for the men, and a tile-covered powder magazine were located inside the stockade. South of the fort was a large building with gardens, a hospital, and a "habitation" (possibly belonging to Benjamin Fooy) with more formal gardens. Near these buildings was the trading post and warehouse of Panton, Leslie, and Company from Mobile. Although it appeared to be carefully conceived and laid out, Fort Gayoso was a difficult post for the Spanish soldiers garrisoned there. In two years of occupation, the fort had four commandants. The jail was usually full, disease was rampant, medical care was unsatisfactory, and food supplies were inadequate. Since there was no lime to make mortar, the military contingent could not construct ovens to bake bread.

Pro-American chief Piomingo and James Colbert's son William (Chooshemataha) led the Chickasaw opposition to the Spanish fort. However, Spanish occupation of the Fourth Bluff and Fort San Fernando was short lived, not so much because of Piomingo's opposition as international relations. Five months after it was completed, Thomas Pinckney, U.S. minister to Great Britain, negotiated a treaty with Spain settling the southern and western boundaries of the United States at the 31st parallel and the Mississippi River. Pinckney's Treaty also recognized the right of United States citizens to navigate the Mississippi River and the right of deposit and transshipment from the port of New Orleans. Spain occupied Fort San Fernando until March 1797, then dismantled the stockade and took some of the logs across the Mississippi River and constructed a smaller fortification at Esperanza, Arkansas. Benjamin Fooy moved his business to this site where he constructed a "vast and handsome residence." But when the city of Memphis was laid out in 1819, Fooy returned to the Fourth Bluff and was given a lot near the site of the house he had occupied at Fort San Fernando.

Spain's influence in the Mississippi Valley ended at the beginning of the nineteenth century. In 1800, they transferred control of the Mississippi River, the Louisiana Territory, and the port of New Orleans back to the French in the Treaty of San Ildefonso. The U.S. government was not immediately aware of the transfer of the Louisiana Territory since Spanish governors continued to serve in New Orleans for several years. However, when French control of the Louisiana Territory and the port of New Orleans became a reality, President Thomas Jefferson authorized a delegation to offer a maximum of $10 million for the port city. Napoleon, faced with war in Europe and difficulty suppressing rebellions on the Caribbean island of Saint-Domingue (Haiti), decided to sell the entire Louisiana Territory to the United States for $15 million.

Isaac Rawlings left the Fourth Bluff soon after his arrival in 1813 or 1814, but returned about ten years later, eventually serving as the second and fourth mayor of Memphis.

Benjamin Fooy warned the Chickasaws that the withdrawal of the Spanish from Fort San Fernando in 1797 would not end their troubles with white settlers; and the Louisiana Purchase marked the beginning of the end of Chickasaw influence at the Fourth Bluff. The tribe was anxious to trade with the Americans for weapons to make war on their enemies, the Creeks, but Americans were as anxious to acquire land as trading rights. The strategic location of the Fourth Bluff was as apparent to the U.S. government as it had been to France, England, and Spain. While visitors to western Tennessee in the late eighteenth century commented on the regal demeanor of the Chickasaws, (English traveler Francis Baily, who visited the area in May 1797, described them as a "well-made, handsome race of men" who welcomed their visitors with "a pipe of peace") they also remarked on the suitability of the Fourth Bluff as a permanent American settlement.[4]

About four months after the Spanish abandoned Fort San Fernando in March 1797, American army Captain Isaac Guion arrived at the Fourth Bluff en route to his post in Natchez. Guion established Fort Adams, named for President John Adams, at the site of the abandoned Spanish fort. The next commandants of Fort Adams were Lieutenant Joseph Campbell and Captain John Pierce (he died a few months after he assumed command of the post). Captain Meriwether Lewis (leader of the Lewis and Clark expedition in 1804–1806), also remained for only a few months. Soon after Lewis left, Fort Adams was abandoned and Fort Pickering, named for then Secretary of State Timothy Pickering, was established 2 miles south of the site. Captain Zebulon Pike, father of the noted nineteenth-century explorer Zebulon M. Pike, became commander of Fort Pickering in October 1800. Pike remained at the fort for nine years before he was replaced by

Lieutenant Zachary Taylor (who, 40 years later, became the twelfth president of the United States). Meriwether Lewis revisited the fort in 1809, and stayed for a few weeks recovering from a serious illness. Lewis, seemingly recovered, left for Washington but was killed or committed suicide on the Natchez Trace.

Fort Pickering served as a "factory" for exchanging pelts and furs brought in by Indian trappers for supplies. The factory system was intended to pull the Indians deeper into debt so that they would be forced to exchange their eastern lands for areas west of the Mississippi River. Early factors included Thomas Peterkin, Peter Morgan, David Hogg, and Robert Bayly. Benjamin Fooy returned to the Fourth Bluff as factor following Bayly's untimely death and was succeeded in 1814 by the most prominent of the nineteenth-century factors, Isaac Rawlings. Rawlings was born in Calvert County, Maryland in 1788, the son of a physician and grandson of a member of the Committee of Safety during the Revolutionary War. Rawlings remained as factor of Fort Pickering until 1816, when he was assigned to set up a new factory for Cherokee Indians who had moved to the Arkansas River. He returned to the Fourth Bluff in the early 1820s and was a leading figure in the development of the city of Memphis.

By the early 1800s, conditions at Fort Pickering had deteriorated. One observer commented that "The post of Chickasaw Bluffs is represented to be unhealthy. What objection can there be to remove, during the summer, the Garrison, leaving a subaltern of discretion with a few men." Other factors complained about the "lawless vending of whiskey and the insolence of the Indians in the absence of a

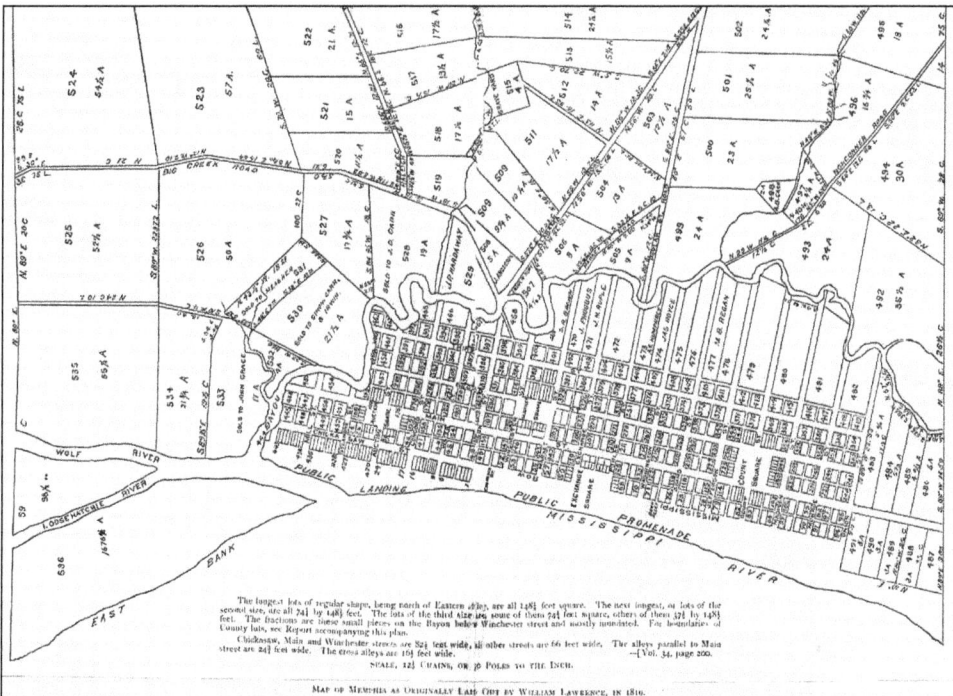

This map of early Memphis is based on an 1819 survey conducted by William Lawrence.

Garrison."[5] The last American troops probably left Fort Pickering in 1813, and the factory system ended in 1822. In 1818, the Chickasaw cession of the northern portion of their lands to the federal government opened the way for more American settlers at the Fourth Bluff. Within ten years the city of Memphis and the county of Shelby were surveyed, laid out, and chartered. What had been an economically and militarily strategic location for Native-American and foreign powers continued to be one of the most important sites on the Mississippi River between St. Louis and New Orleans.

British claims to the Chickasaw Bluffs had been based on the loose boundaries Elizabeth I had assigned to Sir Walter Raleigh's doomed Virginia colony and on Charles II's charter for the Carolina colonies. This charter granted colonial proprietors "title" to lands extending westward from the Atlantic to the Pacific Ocean. After the Revolutionary War, North Carolina claimed the territory from its western boundary to the Mississippi River. The state ceded its claims to the federal government in 1790, but not before dispensing generous land grants to Revolutionary War veterans or selling land to pay war debts. Some of these land sales or grants included territory belonging to the Chickasaws. In October 1783, the land speculators who controlled North Carolina's government opened the Chickasaw lands to purchase. More scrupulous legislators ended the practice seven months later, but by then more

Andrew Jackson, seventh president of the United States, was one of three original proprietors of Memphis.

than half of what was later to become the Western District of Tennessee had been claimed by speculators.

Among the early claimants were John Rice and John Ramsey, who bought title to two adjoining 5,000-acre tracts of land on the Fourth Bluff. These early claimants paid about 5¢ an acre for what would eventually become the heart of downtown Memphis. In 1791, John Rice was killed by Indians near Clarksville, about 10 miles from the Tennessee-Kentucky border. The Rice estate passed to his heirs who eventually sold the Fourth Bluff tract to John Overton and Andrew Jackson. Tennessee became a state on June 1, 1796. The following year, Jackson sold his share to Stephen and Richard Winchester for $625. The two made a quick profit by selling the claim to their brothers, James and William, for $1,000. The original Rice tract now belonged to John Overton (one-half), Andrew Jackson (one-fourth), and William and James Winchester (one-fourth jointly). William Winchester died in 1812, and after the Chickasaw land cession in 1818, Jackson eventually sold his portion to James Winchester for $5,000. An acre of land that cost Rice 5¢ in the 1790s, was now worth $8. The Fourth Bluff, originally part of Washington County, North Carolina, became a part of the state of Tennessee on June 1, 1796, after a census indicated that the population had reached 77,000.

In the second decade of the nineteenth century, there was pressure to open even more Chickasaw land to white settlement. The Tennessee legislature petitioned Congress to relinquish the Chickasaw claim and Congress created a special commission to deal with them. General Jackson was appointed to represent Tennessee and ex-Governor Isaac Shelby to represent Kentucky since the tribe had lands in both states.

The Chickasaws, who at first refused to meet with the commissioners, gave into pressure from Jackson and Shelby and joined in a council at the Chickasaw Old Town site near Aberdeen, Mississippi, in the fall of 1818. The American representatives gained concessions from the Native Americans by intimidation and threats. The Indians agreed to move below the Tennessee-Mississippi border in exchange for $300,000, to be paid in 15 annual installments. The Chickasaws ceded about 6,848,000 acres at approximately 4.5¢ per acre. Surveyors for the presidential commission established the Tennessee's southern boundary with Mississippi and made the Chickasaw Bluffs part of the western boundary. When representatives Levi Colbert and Captain Seely of the Chickasaw Nation, who were part of the commission, complained that surveyors' southern boundary line cut too deeply into the Chickasaw lands, James Winchester, the head of the commission and a proprietary partner in the Rice tract, explained that the instruments used to mark off the land were "more accurate than the path of the sun." Colbert and Seely were not satisfied and left the party to confer with tribal leaders. They later met with Winchester at the Fourth Bluff after he completed the survey. Both declared the line was inaccurate and asked for a resurvey. The Chickasaw Nation lodged a formal protest and worked for ten years to get the boundaries changed.

Protests may have developed when the Chickasaws realized they were giving up the Fourth Bluff. They had no towns or religious shrines in the area, and there were no salt springs or natural resources nearby, but the Fourth Bluff had been an important trading site for centuries. In reality, the Cession line was actually too far north, giving the Chickasaws 440 square miles more than they were entitled to in the treaty. The boundary line was corrected in 1837, after the state of Mississippi had taken title to the rest of the Chickasaw lands.

In 1819, James Winchester recommended that a new county be established in western Tennessee. It was laid out as a rectangle, 30 miles wide by 25 miles long, with the Mississippi River as its western boundary. Winchester, Overton, and Jackson also met at Jackson's Nashville home, the Hermitage, to discuss plans for a new town at the Fourth Bluff. It included 362 lots, broad avenues, four public squares, and a public promenade along the waterfront. Winchester suggested the town be named Memphis. His familiarity with the classics was evidenced in the names he chose for his own children, Marcus, Brutus, Selina, Lucilius, Almire, Napoleon, and Valerius Publicola. Although other American towns were named for the ancient cities—Athens, Rome, Catharge, Corinth—few were named for cities in ancient Egypt. Winchester considered the Mississippi River the American Nile and hoped Memphis on the Mississippi would become a center for trade and culture just as Memphis on the Nile had been. The proprietors ordered maps engraved and took out ads in newspapers advertising their real estate venture. James Winchester's son Marcus and William Lawrence were sent to the Bluff to survey and lay out the town. They completed their work in May 1819, and the first lots were sold to settlers who were already in residence at the site.

Five months later, John Overton petitioned the state legislature for the formation of Shelby County and some county officers were chosen. By the spring of 1820, there were more than 50 people living within the new county of Shelby. At the Fourth Bluff, James Winchester gave his son Marcus a large tract (bordered now by Manassas, Poplar, McNeil, and Union) where the younger Winchester built a store. John Overton encouraged settlement and trade by giving lots to other businessmen for a tavern, a mill, and a tannery. But when other lots were put up for public sale in December 1820, the results were disappointing.

In 1823, Andrew Jackson traded his interest in the Memphis site to James C. McLemore, who was married to Rachel Jackson's niece Elizabeth Donelson, for a tract of land in Madison County. McLemore tried to develop Memphis for the next five years before moving on to another real estate project, the creation of the neighboring town of Fort Pickering, on land he had purchased south of Memphis. Fort Pickering included an Indian trading post, a boat works, factories, a candy plant, and a brewery. It also had a newspaper called the *Eagle* and a boarding school for girls.

Memphis was incorporated by the state of Tennessee on December 9, 1826, over the opposition of some early settlers like Isaac Rawlings, who thought the city had not developed enough wealth or population to need a city government and that supporting a government would be too costly for the poor living in the outskirts of town. Marcus Winchester countered by arguing that incorporation was essential for the town's growth, and proposed that town leaders simply leave the poor in the outskirts. Within two years of incorporation, Rawlings had come on board as a leading proponent of city government. In March 1827, citizens

Located on the east side of Front and north of Overton, a short distance from Marcus Winchester's store, Patrick Meagher's Bell Tavern was a popular resort in the 1820s.

elected the first aldermen: Marcus Winchester, Joseph L. Davis, John Hooke, N.B. Atwood, George F. Graham, John R. Dougherty, and William D. Neely. At their first meeting they chose Winchester as mayor, Rawlings as treasurer, Jacob L. Davis as recorder, and John J. Balch as town constable. The aldermen also passed the town's first ordinances including taxes on lots, all free males between the ages of 21 and 50, all slaves between the ages of 12 and 50, wholesale and retail stores, professionals, tavern keepers, retailers of alcoholic beverages and "stud horses and jacks." The town limits in 1826 were fixed as follows:

> Beginning at the intersection of Wolf River with the Mississippi River; thence with Wolf River to the mouth of Bayou Gayoso; thence with said bayou to the county bridge; thence with the line of the second alley east of, and parallel with Second street to Union street; thence at right angle to Second street to the western boundary of the tract of land entered to John Rice by the grant number 283, dated April 25, 1789; thence with the said western boundary up the Mississippi River to the Wolf River.[6]

In 1828, the original proprietors (Overton, Winchester, and McLemore) gave the city Auction, Market, Exchange, and Court Squares and the waterfront

Marcus Winchester, son of proprietor James Winchester, was the first mayor of Memphis. His first wife, Mary Loiselle, was according to many early commentators a free black woman.

promenade as public grounds. The original charter was amended in 1828, giving the town the same powers as Nashville but providing that the mayor could not hold any office under the federal government. This meant Winchester, who was serving as postmaster, could not be reelected mayor.

Despite the efforts of early settlers and proprietors to encourage the development of Memphis as an economic and political center for southwestern Tennessee, the city faced intense competition from several rivals. Even the state legislature seemed to be working against the town's advancement. When Shelby County was incorporated in 1824, a commission chose a site in the center of the Shelby County at Sanderlin's Bluff, rather than Memphis, as the county seat. The town of Raleigh was then laid out at that site on 29 acres of land purchased from Wilson Sanderlin and 22 acres bought from James Freeman. In 1827, the first court session was held in a newly constructed courthouse. Raleigh became a bustling town and businesses like the Union Inn operated to meet the needs of the permanent and transient population. In 1829, a school for boys opened and was followed eight years later by the Raleigh Female Academy. The original frame courthouse was replaced in the mid-1830s with a two-story brick building.

By the late 1830s, however, Memphis began to surpass Raleigh in economic and political importance. Courts began meeting in Memphis to deal with the criminal element in the growing riverboat town and, as the population increased in the 1840s and 1850s, other judicial and legislative proceedings were organized in the city. It was clear by 1860 that Memphis, not Raleigh, was the political center of Shelby County, a fact supported by the decision to move the county seat to the city. But the Civil War prevented the removal of the government until 1866.

In addition to Fort Pickering and Raleigh, Memphis also contended with the town of Randolph for economic influence during this early period. Randolph was located about 50 miles upriver from Memphis in neighboring Tipton County. It was on the second Chickasaw Bluff at the lower mouth of the Hatchie River, the largest of the four rivers draining west Tennessee into the Mississippi River. Steamboats could travel up the Hatchie as far as Bolivar, Tennessee, and Randolph had a good landing for flatboats. Although Randolph was established after Memphis, by 1829 it had three warehouses, six dry-goods stores, ten physicians, one tavern, and twenty or thirty families. Five years later, New Yorker Francis Latham was publishing a newspaper, the *Randolph Recorder*, and in the 1830s the town had four hotels, nearly fifty businesses, and several private schools, including a college. However, Randolph declined in the late 1830s as a result of several economic and political blows. First, the state legislature chose another town as the county seat for Tipton County. Then a mail line, established in 1829 from Nashville to Memphis, bypassed Randolph and a dispute developed over ownership of the town. Finally, in 1835, a military road was constructed linking Memphis to Little Rock. Randolph's citizens had proposed a canal to connect the Hatchie with the Tennessee River, but Andrew Jackson's opposition to federal support for internal improvements doomed this plan and eventually the city.

In June 1830, Charles-Alexander Le Sueur made this sketch of Young's warehouse, which fronted the Mississippi River just south of the public landing.

3. THE EARLY YEARS

The growth of Memphis as a major economic and political center for the upper Mississippi Valley was tied to cotton, slavery, and to developments in transportation. By the 1830s, cotton cultivation was firmly established in the region. Wagons and small boats brought bales of the fiber to Memphis to be transported to markets downriver and eventually to textile mills in the Northeast and Europe. By the 1850s, Memphis was the "Biggest Inland Cotton Market in the World." On the eve of the Civil War, almost 400,000 bales of cotton left the city's wharves each year.

The expansion of cotton merchandising in Memphis was closely tied to the expansion of slavery in western Tennessee and the Mississippi Delta. In Shelby County, the slave population increased from 103 in 1820 to 16,953 in 1860, when slaves made up just over one-third of the county's total population. Most of this increase was in rural areas outside Memphis. Some farmers and planters had only one or two slaves while others owned hundreds. Even those who owned only a few laborers were invested in the system since they could hire more slave laborers when necessary. In 1860, enslaved African Americans made up 17 percent of Memphis' population. Most worked as mechanics, draymen, assistants to some craftsmen, cooks, washerwomen, and domestic servants.

Slave trading was an important part of the city's economy. One of the best known firms was that of Byrd Hill and Nathan Bedford Forrest. Hill and Forrest and other slave trading establishments like Bolton and Dickens, Zach Curlin, W.E. Eliot, and M.C. Cayce made Memphis the largest slave trading center of any city in the mid-South. Although Tennessee laws prohibited auctions like those common in other slaveholding states, slaves were sold from offices and yards in such frequency that by the 1850s, Memphis was the biggest inland slave market in the South. Newspapers routinely published advertisements for slave sales. For example, J.S. Curtis, an "agent for the sale of and purchase of Negroes and Real Estate," announced the availability of "a number of Negroes, amongst them a fine Cook, Washer and Ironer," to be sold from his office. Curtis noted that he had "large rooms for keeping negroes left with him to sell."[7]

Slave hiring was also important to the city's economy. Memphis merchants advertised the availability of slaves whose labor as cooks, washers, and ironers in urban households, or as agricultural workers could be contracted from their owners. In 1836, the U.S. Army Corps of Engineers hired enslaved men and women to work on the military road under construction between Memphis and the St. Francis River. Slaveholders were paid $22 per month for men and $10–12 per month for women who worked on this project. Workers reportedly received "abundant and wholesome food, good quarters and the best medical attendance . . . provided by the United States."[8]

Most hiring contracts ran from January 1 through December 30, and, in addition to paying the owner for the slave's services, employers were obligated to supply clothing, food, shelter and provide adequate medical care. Each man received a wool hat, a pair of shoes and socks, three shirts, two pair of summer pants and one pair of winter pants, a wool coat, and a blanket. Each woman received two summer dresses and one winter dress, a pair of shoes and woolen stockings, two underdresses, and a blanket.

Not all African Americans in Memphis were enslaved. Although the 1820 and 1830 census omitted them, a small free black population existed in the city from its beginning. This free black population increased from 76 in 1840, to

By 1860, cotton was the principal crop of the mid-South region and African-American slaves represented over one third of the population in Shelby County. But only 17 percent of Memphis' population was black.

Captured fugitive slaves were held in the county jail until their owners came forward to claim them. If unclaimed, the fugitives could be sold at a public auction.

276 in 1860. Tennessee had a strong antislavery movement at the time Memphis and Shelby County were settled and many early residents were not opposed to slaves purchasing their freedom or being freed by their owners. One contemporary stated that a large portion of the money in Marcus Winchester's bank was made up of the small savings of African-American slaves who were trying to buy their freedom. Winchester reportedly deducted the slave's purchase price as well as expenditures for food, clothing, and other necessities, and credited the slave for all their services so that they might eventually purchase freedom. In one instance, two enslaved women, Sarah and Barbara, and their five children were willed to Winchester by J. William Bell with the understanding that Winchester would send them to a free state for manumission. Winchester also had a hand in the emancipation of Ruthie Anna Maria Boyd. In the 1830s, Boyd "prevailed upon one Marcus Winchester to purchase her, under an agreement that he would emancipate her so soon as by the proceeds of her industry she should have re-paid him for the monies expended in her purchase."[9] Winchester later sold Boyd to Jacob N. Moon with the same understanding concerning her freedom, and Boyd was finally freed in January 1850.

The Nashoba community provided another example of the fluidity of race relations and ideas of emancipation in 1820s Memphis and Shelby County. Nashoba was an interracial utopian settlement established by Scottish reformer Frances Wright on a 2,000-acre site in rural Shelby County. It was supported by prominent figures such as Marquis de Lafayette, Robert Owen, Andrew Jackson, and Marcus Winchester who felt the community could become a model for gradual emancipation and black education. Slaves were purchased by or given to the community and employed as field laborers on the plantation, working for wages that were applied toward their purchase price so they could be freed when their full market value was reached. The 2,000-acre tract contained some cotton and corn fields, a few cabins, an orchard, and a school to prepare African Americans for freedom and service as missionaries and colonists in Central and South America.

Life at Nashoba was difficult. In 1826, Wright returned to Europe to recruit new colonists for the Nashoba community. She returned the following year with her friend, English writer Francis Trollope. Trollope was appalled at the primitive state of the community. "One glance sufficed to convince me," Trollope wrote in Domestic Manners of the Americans, "that every idea I had formed of the place was as far as possible from the truth. Desolation was the only feeling, the only word, that presented itself."[10] The sparse diet and shortage of basic necessities hastened Trollope's departure from the community.

Conditions at Nashoba were also compromised by stories of "free love" and "racial mixing." While Frances Wright was in Europe, James Richardson, whom she left in charge (along with her sister Camilla and Richeson Whitby), publicly proclaimed his sexual relationship with a young black woman, Josephine Lalotte, whose mother was a teacher at the Nashoba school. Local residents, who had either supported or ignored the community, were alarmed and condemned it as a "brothel." Nashoba did not recover from these attacks and Frances Wright ended her emancipation experiment by arranging for the Nashoba slaves to be transported to Haiti, where they were freed and given land by the Haitian government.

In the 1840s, Memphis was already a city in "black and white," where African Americans, slave and free, worked alongside or under the supervision of white employers as in this drawing of Mississippi Row (Front Street).

Memphians became increasingly intolerant of interracial relationships. Although Tennessee outlawed interracial marriages in 1822, a few slave and free black women lived as "housekeepers," "concubines," or common-law wives of white men. Marcus Winchester, the city's first mayor, was reportedly married to Marie Loiselle, a free black woman from St. Louis. The couple had eight children before her death. Contemporaries emphasized Marie's acts of charity and support for religious work and described her as a woman of "exemplary and unobtrusive deportment," who, except for the matter of her race, could have been a "lady." Winchester and Loiselle were also friends of Frances Wright. But by 1830s, Memphians were less tolerant of interracial liaisons, especially those that seemed to allow black women equal status with white women. In 1837, a city ordinance specifically prohibited white men from "keeping colored wives."

The legal status of free blacks in Tennessee deteriorated in the three decades before the Civil War. Until the 1830s, free black men possessed many of the same legal rights as their white neighbors, including the right to vote and public education. Most free blacks were manual laborers, craftsmen, or domestic workers. In Memphis, free black women and men, like Millie Swan and Joseph Clouston, owned property, participated in black religious congregations, and helped organize mutual aid societies. Yet changes in the Tennessee constitution, new state laws, and local ordinances reduced or eliminated some rights of free blacks. Their economic opportunities and interactions with slaves were restricted. Slaves were prohibited from hiring their own time and arranging their own housing in the city, and free blacks had to register with the county court and pay a bond to remain in the community.

By the 1850s, Memphis was the trading center for the agricultural hinterland. Cotton factors acted as financial intermediaries. They provided capital in the form of seed and other provisions to farmers and planters until crops were harvested. The first private banks opened in the city in the early 1830s. The Farmers and Merchants Bank, located at the corner of Jefferson and Front Streets, opened in 1833, the Union Bank in 1839, and Planters Bank in 1842. In the 1850s, 11 new banks opened. However, three banks, including the Farmers and Merchants, failed in the 1850s, as did several others during the Civil War and Reconstruction period.

Antebellum business interests in the city were primarily retail and wholesale outlets. In 1849 there were 31 dry goods merchants, 40 grocery and commission merchants, 44 lawyers, and 25 doctors, but there were no large-scale manufacturing establishments in the city. Ninety-three businesses produced items like boots and shoes, wagons and carts, steam engines, tin, copper and sheet iron, saddlery, and harnesses.

Developments in transportation and communication were important to commerce and agriculture in the region. Before 1820 there was no access to the city by way of public roads. Indian trials were the principal means of communication and transportation between the city and areas further east. In

Frances Wright planned her 1820s Nashoba community as a model for gradual emancipation of slaves.

1820, several early settlers were ordered by the county court to mark out a road from the town north to the county line in the direction of a settlement on the Forked Deer River. The following year, another road was laid out from the city north to a settlement on Big Creek and Loosahatchie and on to the Forked Deer River settlement. In 1829, tri-weekly postal service was established by four-horse coaches from Nashville through Jackson, Bolivar, Somerville, Raleigh, and on to Memphis. These roads encouraged settlement along their routes and increased trade and commerce with Memphis.

Passenger transportation from Memphis also stimulated the city's economy and encouraged migration. In 1831, stagecoaches began operating from Memphis through Jackson to Nashville. Post and stage routes, as well as public roads, extended rapidly after that date. Property owners, their tenants, and slaves were required to work on roads adjacent to their properties. Although these dirt paths were impassable during the spring rains, they were the only inland access to the river until 1845, when charters were issued for the construction of turnpikes and plank roads. The first of these, the Memphis and Somerville Road, was chartered in 1846 and re-chartered the following year. The Pigeon Roost and Chulahoma Road was chartered in 1853, and the Memphis and Horn Lake Road was chartered the following year. But turnpikes were difficult to maintain because of the region's sandy soil and plank roads were expensive to repair. Most fell into disrepair during the Civil War and their charters were dissolved in 1866. An 1875 state law, which allowed counties to build turnpikes using convict labor, enabled

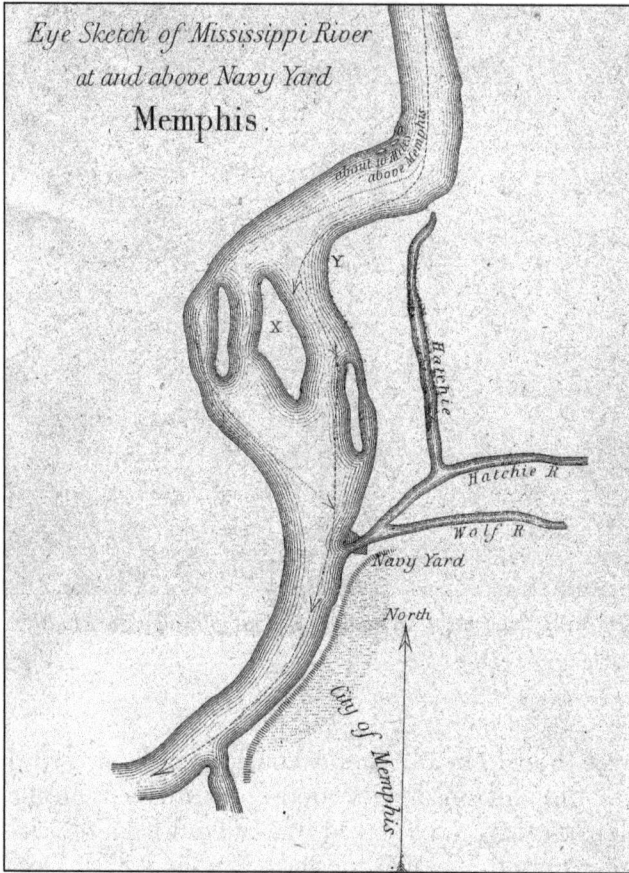

Eye Sketch of Mississippi River
at and above Navy Yard
Memphis.

Supporters of the Memphis Navy Yard thought that its central, inland location provided a means of protecting the western rivers and the Gulf of Mexico.

Shelby County to improve its road system. Eight years later the state legislation also allowed tax levies for road construction.

Efforts to tie Memphis to the trans-Mississippi west began soon after the city was incorporated. In 1826, Congress authorized construction of a military road from the west bank of the river to Little Rock. Construction was difficult and the project languished for several years. The first leg of the road crossed swamps extending 38 miles into Arkansas and in the spring the road was often underwater as deep as 18 feet.

The Memphis Navy Yard gave Memphians another opportunity to promote the city's strategic location. Supporters noted that the city's position on the bluffs was ideal for protecting the South and the West. The Mississippi River was navigable year round from Memphis south to the Gulf of Mexico. A navy yard at Memphis could also draw supplies from the Ohio and the Mississippi Valleys. After three years of lobbying, the federal government finally agreed to the idea and paid the city $25,000 for a waterfront location at the mouth of the Wolf River between Auction and Market Streets. But the site was less advantageous than it seemed. The discovery of quicksand underneath the soil forced the government to limit plans for the installation.

Instead of a full-scale shipyard with heavy dock machinery, the Memphis Navy Yard was restricted to outfitting of masts and rigging; and the only major vessel on record as having been outfitted at the yard was the *Alleghany*, which was completed in 1847. The *Alleghany* was the first all-iron ship built for naval service. Its hull was constructed in Pittsburgh, Pennsylvania, and towed to Memphis, where the vessel was rigged, masted, and fitted. After six years in service off the coast of Brazil and in the Mediterranean Ocean, the *Alleghany* was remodeled, then decommissioned and sold in 1869. Criticisms of the limited operations of the Memphis Navy Yard eventually led Tennessee Senator James J. Jones to suggest that Congress either support the venture or give it back to the city. The federal government chose the latter option and returned the site to the city in 1854. Memphis leaders later pledged land as security for another transportation project, the construction of the Memphis and Little Rock Railroad.

As the nation moved from the era of road building to the age of railroads, settlers in western Tennessee supported developing rail transportation in the region. In 1835, businessmen in Memphis and La Grange (east of the city in neighboring Fayette County) got a charter to build a railroad between the two towns. Funding came from subscriptions and construction began in 1838. Four years later, only 6 miles of track had been constructed. The railroad was never completed and was declared a total failure. From 1848 to 1850, Governor James J. Jones proposed the construction of a railroad line from Memphis to

The Navy Yard was originally planned as a full-scale ship yard, but the discovery of quicksand at the site limited its use to fitting vessels with masts and rigging.

Charleston, South Carolina. The Memphis and Charleston Railroad Company had purchased the charter of the Memphis and La Grange Company. Work began in 1850, but it was not completed until eight years later. To symbolize the uniting of the Atlantic Ocean with the Mississippi River, the first train from Charleston carried a hogshead of ocean water to pour into the river and the first train from Memphis to Charleston carried a hogshead of river water to pour into the ocean.

Another railroad line, the Memphis branch of the Louisville and Nashville, was chartered in 1852 as the Memphis and Nashville Railroad. The line ran northeast from the city to connect with the main line at Bowing Green. The Mississippi and Tennessee Railroad was also chartered in 1852. The city bought $250,000 of the stock and the state of Tennessee loaned the company $97,500. The 100-mile long railroad, completed in 1857, stretched from Memphis to Grenada, Mississippi, and connected with the Illinois Central line (then called the Mississippi Central Railroad). More importantly, this railroad line linked farms in the rich Mississippi Delta to Memphis, where steamboats carried crops to New Orleans and on to mills and factories in the northeast and Europe.

The Memphis and Little Rock Railroad was chartered in 1853 but took 20 years to complete. Memphis subscribed $350,000 and the federal government donated 487,000 acres of land in Arkansas along the route. Goods brought into Memphis were probably ferried across the river to the railroad terminal on the other side. From there, the railroad extended 135 miles into Arkansas, linking with other railroad lines to reach the Pacific Ocean. A bridge across the river was not completed for another 40 years.

As Memphis grew in population, commerce, and size, city leaders began to explore the possibilities for cheap, efficient transportation within the city and between the city and suburban communities. By 1860, Memphis was the sixth largest city in the South. In June 1865, the Memphis City Railroad Company was incorporated, and within a year it had constructed lines from Jackson Street, near the Mississippi and Tennessee Depot, along Main to the Louisville and Nashville Depot; from Main at Poplar Street to the Boulevard; from Main at Beale, Lauderdale, and Vance streets to a point opposite St. Agnes Academy (on Vance near Orleans); and from Main on Jefferson to the Memphis and Charleston Depot. The lines covered a distance of 10 miles. The initial fare of 5¢ doubled the following year to 10¢, but was eventually reduced to 6 1/4¢ and, in 1875, reduced again to the original fare of 5¢. In 1872, the railway line was extended to Kerr Street in Chelsea, and three years later from Main and Vance to Estival Park.

A second railway company, the Citizens' Railway Company, was chartered in 1885 to build a line from Fort Pickering on Shelby, Front, and Madison Streets and Johnson Avenue to Estival Park; from Cole's Mills out on Hernando Road along Hernando, Union, Second, Winchester, Alabama, and other streets to Scotland; and from Elmwood Cemetery along Linden, Hernando, Union, Second, and other streets to Leath Orphan Asylum on the Raleigh Road. The line was completed in the fall of 1886. Rivalry between the two companies began almost as soon as the Citizen's Railway completed its road. The two eventually merged into a single railway line with 40 miles of track and 225 workers, and the new company extended the Shelby Street line (in Fort Pickering) to the old Indian mounds. Streets were paved where the new tracks were laid and new, large cars were put into service. Napoleon Hill, one of the founders of the Citizen's Railway Company, became the president of the consolidated company. In 1887, the Memphis, Greenwood and Prospect Park Railroad Company constructed transit lines between the city and the suburbs.

By the late nineteenth century, streetcars shared public streets with horse-drawn carriages, pedestrians, and dray wagons.

4. Boom Times on the Bluff

In the early 1800s, most black and white migrants to Memphis came from Virginia, the Carolinas, Georgia, or from the mid-South, the broad expanse of rich farmland bordering the Mississippi River that includes western Tennessee, eastern Arkansas, northern Mississippi and Alabama, and southern Missouri. The addition of thousands of Irish and German immigrants in the 1840s made Memphis one of the most diverse and populous cities in the South. By 1850, Irish immigrants were 9.9 percent of the city's population while German immigrants were 5.3 percent. Ten years later, Irish immigrants were 23.2 percent and German immigrants were 9 percent. Enslaved and free African Americans were 28 percent of the population in 1850, but only 17 percent in 1860.

Memphis grew slowly in the first two decades of its existence because of commercial rivalry with its neighbors. But by 1840, Memphis was a bustling western city. Fifty years later, a resident reminisced about Memphis at mid-century:

> The main portion of the town lay back of Poplar street, skirted by the bayou on the east and north, with its front mainly on Wolf River. The only cut down the bluff was at Market street, another at Auction, where it tapered off to a hill some fifteen feet high, and terminated at the alley north of Sycamore street. A view from the deck of a steamer, south of Market street, presented a continuous high fronting bluff, just such as can now be seen south of Beal street. Winchester street was then the centre of the town. The city hotel was located on the southwest corner of Winchester and Main, fronting the former; the Farmers' and Merchant's Bank on the diagonal corner opposite, fronting Main, in the brick building still standing, but remodeled a few years ago. One drug store was opposite the hotel, another on the south side of Winchester, near Mississippi Row (now Front Street). The principal saloon and restaurant was on the northeast corner of Winchester and Front alley in the large two-story frame building, still standing there. There were several stores on Mississippi Row, south of Winchester, as far as market street, and perhaps to Exchange, also others north of Winchester on Jackson, on which corner was

the post office. From Jackson, south and west of Mississippi Row, was the open promenade, but north of Jackson the street called Chickasaw was built up on both sides, mostly stores, as far north as Overton street.[11]

From its establishment in the early 1800s, Memphis welcomed one religious group after another. In the 1820s, itinerant circuit riding ministers traveled to the Fourth Bluff to preach to mixed congregations of Baptists, Methodists, Presbyterians, and other denominations. Circuit riding ministers traveled on horseback making regular stops at isolated cabins and small settlements. They were paid a yearly stipend of $80–$100 for their services. They held meetings in "brush arbors," a practice that continued into the twentieth century.

Harry Lawrence was one of the earliest of the itinerant ministers who preached on the Bluff. Lawrence was an African-American minister whose sermons attracted mixed audiences. Other early ministers included Elijah Coffee, a "True-Will Baptist" who also preached to other denominations, and Silas Toncray, a "Hard-shell Baptist," who built his own church and organized a congregation of slaves and free blacks. After Toncray's death, the black congregation became the African Church, the city's first black church. For most of the city's early ministers, preaching was a part-time activity. Coffey was also a shoemaker, and the city's mayor; Toncray was a silversmith, watchmaker, engraver, druggist, dentist, and alderman.

From the 1820s to the 1860s, thousands of German and Irish immigrants arrived in the Memphis area.

More formalized congregations emerged by the end of the 1820s, although religious groups often shared facilities until they could build their own separate edifices. Charles Locke's house on Front Street between Concord and Second was used alternately by Baptists, Methodists, and Presbyterians. In 1830, Presbyterians moved their services across the street from the Locke house to the Schabell house. In 1826, Methodist minister T.P. Davidson organized the First Methodist Church. The congregation met in a building near the mouth of the Wolf River until they purchased land from Marcus Winchester and erected the first church building in Memphis. The church, also called Wesley Chapel, began with only 11 members, but an early revival soon brought the membership total to 60.

First Presbyterian Church, organized in 1828 with five members, met in a schoolhouse on Court Square until 1834, when a church building was erected at the corner of Third and Poplar. Ten years later, Second Presbyterian Church was organized and this congregation dedicated its building at Main and Beale in 1848. The First Baptist Church congregation erected a building on Second between Adams and Washington. The first Episcopal services in the city were held on a flatboat in 1832. Between 1835 and 1865, four Episcopal Churches were organized: Calvary Church in 1835, St. Mary's Cathedral in 1857, Grace Church in 1853, and the Church of the Good Shepard in 1865.

The city's Catholic population was small until the 1840s and 1850s. Father Stokes said the first Catholic masses at the home of Eugene Magevney on Adams and at Magevney's schoolhouse. There were no regular services until 1841. Three years later St. Peter's Church was erected on Third Street near Adams.

Front Street was a bustling business district in the decades before and after the Civil War.

Dominican friars began serving the parish in 1845. St. Mary's Catholic Church originated among a society of German Catholics who had been worshipping at St. Peter's. A small wooden house at the corner of Third and Market Streets was outfitted as a church and school and, in 1860, a resident pastor joined the congregation. Ten years later, Franciscan fathers began ministering to the parish. In the mid-1860s, St. Patrick's Church was organized to serve Catholics in the southeastern part of the city. Services were held in the parsonage near the schoolhouse until the church building was completed. In the late nineteenth century, two more Catholic churches opened, St. Bridged's on the corner of Third and Overton, and St. Joseph's on the corner of Georgia and Seventh. Like St. Peter's and St. Mary's, St. Joseph's was identified with a particular immigrant group in the city—in this case Italians.

Among the other Protestant churches established in the nineteenth century were Linden Avenue Christian Church (organized in 1846 with a building at the corner of Linden and Mulberry), the German Evangelical Lutheran Trinity Church (organized in 1855 with a building constructed the next year on Washington Avenue), and the Stranger's Church (organized in 1863 as the First Congregational Church with a building on Union Avenue). The Congregation of the Children of Israel was formed in 1854. The congregation received $2,000 from the estate of Judah Touro of New Orleans to build their synagogue. They purchased a lot on Second Street, but services were held in the old Farmers' and Merchants Bank building until 1884 when a temple was erected on Poplar.

Antebellum African-American slaves and free blacks worshiped in homes, with white congregations, or as separate congregations in white churches. An early visitor who stumbled on a religious gathering of blacks in early Memphis:

> In a lone house, in a lane, I heard the sound of psalm-singing, about eleven o'clock at night, and stopped to listen to a tune. . . . The psalm ceased, and a Negro slave delivered a long extempore prayer like those of the Presbyterians, and using excellent language. The prayer was followed by a sermon. . . . The audience consisted of a few men and women, sitting on forms in a loft, lighted by a solitary candle. [12]

Other black Memphians attended white churches where they stood in the back or sat in segregated sections, yet in several cases the number of African-American members was large enough to form a separate congregation within the churches. At First Presbyterian Church, African Americans held daily sunrise prayer meetings and separate services in the church's basement. The African American Presbyterian Church even raised funds to repair and beautify their basement section. At Wesley Chapel, a free black man, Daniel Jones, preached to slaves and free blacks who constituted the African Mission that met in the church's basement. In 1859, the African Mission established the independent Collins Chapel Church, named for the white minister who took over after Daniel Jones died. In the 1860s, black congregations in the city left white facilities to construct their own separate edifices. Black Baptists established the Colored Baptist Church with Moses Henderson, a former slave, as their pastor. The members held services in a brush arbor while they raised money to purchase a lot at the corner of Beale and DeSoto. Their church, Beale Street Baptist or First Colored Baptist, was the first brick structure owned by African Americans in Memphis. By the end of the century, African Americans had organized Baptist, Christian, Presbyterian, Episcopal, Congregational, and Methodist congregations throughout the city.

Although there are casual references to private schools, there is little evidence of any schools until the second decade of Memphis history. Most were separated by gender and age group, and were taught by men and women in buildings also used for other purposes. The first of these private schools was organized by a Mr. Garner in 1831 in an old building near the northeast corner of Chickasaw and Auction Streets. Later, two other men opened a school in a building near the middle of Court Square that was originally used as a church by several different denominations before they built their own independent edifices. Another pioneering teacher in the city was Eugene Magevney, who opened a school for boys in a building also used for public meetings, church services, and political gatherings.

Although the 1826 city charter provided for public schools, the first tax-supported public educational institution was not established until June 19, 1848, when Colonel J.W.A. Pettit, an alderman, was authorized to build a school in his ward at the corner of Third and Overton. The school was later moved to the Methodist Church and schools were soon established in the other two wards. Pettit was eventually elected superintendent of schools, an unpaid position until 1850. City schools were incorporated by an 1856 state law that made white children six to twenty years old, living within the city limits, eligible for admission to free schools. Others could be admitted on payment of tuition, but city ordinances prohibited Sabbath Schools that were the principal means of education for slave or free black children. One writer argued that, "letter instruction to slaves is dangerous in a high degree, [since] however excellent a thing it may be for the slave to read the Bible, it is by no means probable that his reading will be confined to that."[13] Memphis property holders were assessed a school tax, which free African Americans were not required to pay.

The Civil War interrupted free school education throughout the South, but in Memphis school enrollment dropped only slightly. The major development in public education in the 1860s concerned the education of African-American men, women, and children. The first teachers in schools for African Americans were men and women associated with Union army units stationed in the city or missionary teachers working in the three contraband camps in or near Memphis. In 1862, Lucinda Humphrey opened an evening school for African-American hospital attendants. The following year, Humphrey and two other white women were assigned to a school, funded by Union army officers and the black

Located at the corner of Beale and Fourth, Historic Beale Street Baptist Church is one of the oldest African-American congregations in Memphis.

community, in a contraband camp. Fannie Kiddo, a white missionary teacher supported by the United Presbyterian Aid Society, opened another school in early 1863. In the same year the American Missionary Association (AMA) sponsored a school run by T.H. Place, a former Union soldier, in the basement of the Baptist Church on Beal Street.

For most of the Civil War and Reconstruction period, teachers in African-American schools in Memphis, as in other parts of the South, were white missionaries. However, independent schoolrooms were also housed in and operated by African-American churches or private individuals. Two black women, identified only as Miss Cooper and Miss R.N. Stewart, worked in a school operated by Stewart's father, Reverend Thomas N. Stewart. In another instance, Celia Burton Burris, an antebellum free black woman, leased space in her home

The log cabin in Court Square was used as a school house by Professor Eugene Magevney as well as for public meetings, church services, and political gatherings.

to the Freedmen's Bureau to operate a school. Yet there was no formal public system for educating African Americans until 1864 when missionary schools were incorporated into the city school system. By 1865, nearly 2,000 black students attended schools in Memphis. In May 1866, all black school or church buildings were destroyed in a brutal three-day race riot. The schools and churches were quickly rebuilt and by the end of 1870, there were 15,421 African-American students out of a total 42,226 students in city schools. Although schools were racially segregated, for the next five years the faculties in the African-American schools were made up of black and white teachers. More black teachers were hired and, in July 1875, the school board appointed a black man, B.K. Sampson, principal of one of the African-American schools. For the next century, only black teachers were employed in black schools.

By 1888, the city had five public schools for blacks and by the end of the century many of the teachers in these schools were products of the school system. However, others were recent migrants to the city. Journalist and activist Ida B. Wells came to Memphis from Holly Springs, Mississippi, in the 1880s and taught in the rural schools of Shelby County as well as Memphis. Olivia Davidson, who later became Booker T. Washington's second wife and a fundraiser for Tuskegee Institute in Alabama, also taught in the city schools during the mid-1870s.

In the 1870s, the city also began constructing more substantial public schoolhouses for white students. In 1871, Smith School, which one historian described as "the city's first public school-house in Memphis, worthy [of] the name," was constructed at Market and Third. It was a three-story, brick structure with 12 classrooms, a principal's office, and library rooms. Peabody School was built in 1872 and Clay Street School (for African-American students) was erected in 1874. Construction of school buildings waned in the late 1870s in the aftermath of two deadly yellow fever epidemics, but in the 1880s, Grant, Porter, and Pope Schools were added to the system.

Private and select schools and colleges also dotted the city's educational landscape from the 1840s. The first college was a branch of Union University of Tennessee, built in 1843 by B.F. Farnsworth. The institution lasted only a few years before Farnsworth returned to his home in Kentucky. The oldest private school in the city was St. Agnes Female Academy, established in 1851 by Father T.L. Grace. Father Grace purchased the "Coe Place" on Vance, near Orleans, for the school. The original building was destroyed by fire in 1878, but a new structure was built the next year. The State Female College was constructed in 1858 at the corner of McLemore and College Avenues. During the Civil War, the college buildings and grounds were occupied by federal troops and were the site of a fierce firefight during N.B. Forrest's raid into Memphis. The school resumed operations after the war, but had not fully recovered when the yellow fever epidemic struck the city. The school eventually closed, although one building housed a private school for girls run by Memphian Mollie Marshall.

Many other private schools and colleges opened in the late nineteenth century. The LeMoyne Institute was established in 1871 by the American Missionary Association to educate African Americans, and benefited from a donation by Dr. F. Julius LeMoyne of Pennsylvania. Buildings were constructed on Orleans Street and the school opened in September 1871. The institution trained many of the

Founded in 1858, the State Female College was among the most successful early educational institutions in the city.

43

black teachers for the city's public schools and sent other students on to colleges and universities throughout the south.

In 1877, veteran teachers Jenny M. Higbee and Clara Conway opened schools for white females. "Miss Higbee's High School" was originally housed in the old St. Mary's school building on Poplar Street, but three years later, the school moved to the old Robertson Topp mansion at the intersection of Beale and Lauderdale. The school offered a secondary school program for girls that included English, natural sciences, literature, ancient and modern languages, music, painting, and wood carving. The Clara Conway Institute was also located on Poplar Street. The Institute operated the first kindergarten in Memphis and taught freehand drawing, gymnastics, and physical culture as well as elocution, English literature, and other subjects.

Newspapers reflected the racial, religious, and ethnic diversity as well as the social, political, and economic development of the city. Memphis papers promoted a sense of identity among diverse groups, but also reflected the cosmopolitan nature of city life. The first newspaper, the *Memphis Advocate and Western District Intelligencer*, appeared in 1827, six years after the town was laid out. It was followed four years later by the *Western Times and Memphis Commercial Advertiser*. The two papers merged soon after into the *Times and Advocate*, but the union lasted only a year. The *Times* folded soon afterward and the *Advocate* ended publication in 1835. By this time, the city had three other papers, the *Memphis Gazette* (an organ of the Democratic party), the *Memphis Enquirer*, and the *Memphis Intelligencer*. The publisher of the *Enquirer*, F.S. Latham, purchased the *Intelligencer*, and by 1847 the former *Enquirer* (a Whig paper) was issued as a daily paper. In 1851, it merged with the city's other Whig publication, the *Memphis Daily Eagle*, to form the *Enquirer and Eagle*. When it was sold ten years later to the publishers of the *Memphis Avalanche*, it ended its run as the city's oldest newspaper after being published under various names in one form or another for 25 years.

The *Enquirer*'s principal rival in the 1840s was Henry Van Pelt's *Memphis Appeal*. It developed from the *Western World and Memphis Banner of the Constitution*, which circulated in 1839. Van Pelt changed its name and made it one of the leading Democratic Party newspapers in the South and the West and in 1849 the paper began publishing daily issues. Edward Pickett became editor after Van Pelt's death in 1851, and the publication expanded over the next three years "to keep pace with the advancement of the times."[14]

Before Memphis fell to the Union Army on June 6, 1862, the *Appeal*'s type, presses, and other equipment were loaded into a boxcar and moved first to Grenada, Mississippi, then to Montgomery, Alabama, and finally to Atlanta, Georgia. Under the banner of the *Memphis Daily Appeal*, the newspaper's editors continued to publish articles that supported secession and the Confederacy as it moved from city to city. After the fall of Atlanta, the paper moved to Columbus, Georgia, where it was seized by Union soldiers and the editor was arrested. At the end of the war, the *Appeal* was brought back to Memphis. The *Memphis Daily*

LeMoyne Institute was established in 1871 by the American Missionary Association.

Argus, an anti-war journal, was published in the city from 1859 to 1866. From 1865 to 1870, the *Memphis Post*, a Republican Party newspaper, published daily, tri-weekly, and weekly issues. Other newspapers included the *Memphis Avalanche*, the *Public Ledger*, and the *Memphis Scimitar*.

Memphis also boasted an array of newspapers dedicated to the views and interests of particular religious, literary, social, ethnic, and economic groups. The city's large population of German immigrants had ethnic newspapers from the mid-1850s. The first of these was *Die Stimme die Volk* (1854–1860), followed by *Der Anzieger des Sudens* (1858–1876). The *Memphis Journal* was a German newspaper published by Charles Weidt from August 1876 until Weidt left the city during the 1876 yellow fever epidemic. Weidt later sold it to the owners of the *Southern Post Journal*. The *German Gazette* and the *Memphis Democrat* were also published in the late nineteenth century.

The migration of thousands of African Americans into Memphis during and after the Civil War, and the development of African-American schools, created an audience for black newspapers. At least four were established in Memphis between the 1870s and the 1890s. The first of these, the *Mississippi Baptist*, was published by C.C. Dickinson between 1872 and 1883. It appeared as a semi-weekly between 1872 and 1876; in 1876, the newspaper became a weekly. In the 1870s, Alfred Froman, a veteran of the African-American Civil War regiment the Fifty-Fourth Massachusetts, also published *The Weekly Planet*. In 1883, Dickinson sold his paper and it was renamed the *Memphis Watchman*. W.A. Brinkley and R.N. Countee began publishing *The Living Way* in 1874. *The Living Way* and the *Memphis Watchman* were rival newspapers.

Ida B. Wells, who was working in the city's African-American schools in the mid-1880s, considered working for Countee's paper, but he was unwilling to make her a paid correspondent. Instead, in 1889, Wells joined the city's newest newspaper, the *Free Speech and Headlight*, owned by Reverend Taylor Nightingale and J.L. Fleming and published in the basement of Nightingale's Beale Street Baptist Church. Wells bought a one-third interest in the newspaper and eventually became its editor. Two years later she became a full-time journalist when she was not rehired as a teacher after writing and publishing articles criticizing conditions in black schools. Nightingale withdrew from the newspaper and the office moved to Hernando Street near Beale Street. Wells' fiery criticisms of African-American lynchings, including the murders of three black businessmen in Memphis in 1892, led to the destruction of the paper's offices. Wells, who was out of the city at the time, did not return and eventually settled in Chicago.

Temperance groups, labor unions, farmers, and planters also published their own papers in nineteenth-century Memphis. The first temperance newspaper, the *Family Visitor*, appeared in the 1840s. One observer noted that it was a very influential publication for the time. Forty years later, Reverend D.D. Moore published a weekly temperance paper, the *Standard*. From the mid-1860s to the late nineteenth century, agricultural interests published at least five newspapers. The first was a monthly journal, the *Southern Farmer*, which began publication in 1865 and continued until 1874 or 1875. In 1872, three papers began publication but none lasted more than a year. Grangers began the weekly *Patron of Husbandry* in 1877, but the paper dissolved before the end of the decade. Trade unionists published the *Memphis Mercury* from 1883 to 1886.

During the first two decades of the city's existence, law enforcement was left to part-time city marshals or constables. In 1845, two regular patrolmen were assigned to day and night shifts; two more officers were added the following year. The number of policemen increased to between 12 and 16 by 1850. A city marshal, chosen by the mayor and with the same powers as a chief of police, administered this police force. In 1866, the state legislature created three-man Metropolitan Police Commissions for Memphis, Nashville, and Chattanooga. Policemen worked 12-hour day or night shifts, but were paid on time and in cash. In the 1880s, police facilities were generally inadequate. There was only one station house, located first on Adams Street and later on Second Street. Like police departments in other Southern cities, the Memphis police force included African Americans from the 1860s to the 1890s. In the late 1860s, eight blacks served as jailers and two as detectives, but by the mid-1870s, the number of black policemen dropped to three turnkeys and an assistant station house keeper. Two left after a few months and by mid-1875, there were no blacks on the police force.

African Americans were called back to duty during the 1878 yellow fever epidemic when many regular policemen left the city or succumbed to the

The Shelby County Jail could comfortably house up to 350 prisoners in a facility that had steam heat, an exercise yard, bathhouses, a washroom, a detached kitchen, and a water tower.

disease. By the early 1880s, the numbers dropped again after the forced reorganization of the city government under the Taxing District Act. By 1882, there were only five black policemen and the last African-American constable of the nineteenth century retired in 1895.

As in other cities, Memphis firemen operated as volunteer companies with their own engines until 1859. The first company was organized in 1829 and purchased "Little Vigor" soon afterward. The quality of fire service was so poor that, as one historian noted, "a house never caught fire but it burned down."[15] The problems stemmed from poor equipment and an inadequate water supply. Firemen had to haul their engines to the scene of the fire by ropes, then break into neighboring yards to get water. The fact that they often drained a cistern in the process made the fire companies unpopular with many city residents. In 1859, the city began paying firemen and, the following year, purchased the first engine, "J.B. Danbury." Two more engines were purchased during the Civil War, although the city had a difficult time keeping men on the payroll as many left to join the Confederate Army and the fire engines were confiscated for the war effort.

By 1860, there were six newspapers, twenty Baptist, Methodist, Presbyterian, and Catholic churches, one synagogue, numerous private schools, three female seminaries, and two medical schools in Memphis. Twenty-one tax-supported public schoolrooms operated in the city. The city also boasted two private orphanages, branches of the Young Men's Christian Association, and numerous Bible and temperance societies. Memphians enjoyed musical, operatic, and dramatic productions at Crisp's Gaiety, the New Memphis Theater, and the

Gayoso House and other hotels housed visitors. Gas lamps were installed on city streets in the 1850s and a mule-drawn streetcar system began operating in 1860. But the city fell short in its efforts to cope with problems in road improvements, sanitation, public health and debt management. In spite of its semblance of urbanity, Memphis was still a town dominated by the rural economy of the hinterland and the rural background and values of the men and women who migrated to the city. Even in the late nineteenth century, one historian described the city as one of the most "rural" cities in the South.

The first volunteer fire company was organized in the latter part of 1829, and a paid fire department was established in 1859.

5. THE CIVIL WAR CITY

The Civil War was a watershed event in Memphis history. Before the war, African Americans constituted 17 percent of the city's population. All but 198 of the nearly 4,000 blacks in the city were enslaved. By 1865, African Americans comprised 39 percent of the population; all were now free either as a result of government proclamation, personal action, or the passage of the 13th Amendment to the Constitution. Although the city experienced little of the physical destruction the Civil War wreaked on Atlanta and Vicksburg, military occupation and changes in the population dramatically altered the social, political, and economic climate in Memphis.

Tennessee was a reluctant addition to the Confederacy. In the months preceding and immediately after Abraham Lincoln's victory in the 1860 presidential election, Memphians were no less ambivalent in their support. The *Memphis Enquirer* called secession a "madman's remedy" and the *Memphis Appeal* called attention to the importance of Northern-made products to the city's economy. In November 1860, only one out of every eight Memphians favored secession. As Memphian Elizabeth Avery Meriwether noted, "When news of South Carolina's secession reached Memphis everybody was stunned; Tennesseans did not want to quit the Union," and, despite their support of South Carolina's action and their opposition the Republican Party, "they did not think it wise or necessary to secede."[16] Initially, most Memphians felt Lincoln's election would have little impact on the city's economy or the agricultural hinterland Memphis depended upon. Some even suggested the secession of some Deep South states would enhance the city's position as a trading center for the upper South and the Midwest.

Between November and April, both unionists and secessionists lobbied public opinion at rallies, churches, saloons, and other gatherings or in the city's newspapers. But local sentiment gradually turned toward secession. The failures of the Crittenden Compromise and the Washington Peace Conference, the attack on Fort Sumter, and Lincoln's call for soldiers galvanized public sentiment in favor of the Confederacy. By April 1861, the Memphis population was overwhelmingly supportive of the Confederacy. At the largest public meeting in its history up to that point, Memphians resolved to leave the Union. Citizens began organizing militia units like the Garibaldi Guards, the Emerald Guards, the Bluff City Greys, the Shelby Greys, the Crockett Rangers, and the Mounted Riflemen. Merchants Leo Ketchum and G.D. Jones organized a battalion of 500 men, and surviving soldiers of the War of 1812 joined another group organized by survivors of the 1848 Mexican War.

Women encouraged their husbands and sons to join the Confederate Army. In a letter to the *Memphis Appeal*, female supporters declared that "though we cannot bear arms, yet our hearts are with you, and our hands are at your service to make clothing, flags, or anything that a patriotic woman can do for the Southern men and Southern Independence."[17] The association of "Southern Mothers" was also organized in late April.

Even before Tennessee seceded from the federal union, Governor Isham Harris began making preparations to join the Confederacy. In February, Major General Samuel R. Anderson was ordered by Harris to organize volunteer forces in western Tennessee. On May 7, Harris entered a military agreement with the Confederacy and Major General Gideon J. Pillow was sent to erect batteries along the Mississippi River above Memphis as a part of Confederate fortifications along the river. Confederate president Jefferson Davis also established a recruiting headquarters in the city and Memphis received support from other seceding states. The state of Louisiana sent a battery of 32-pound guns, 3,000 Mississippi rifles, and half a million cartridges. Quimby and Robinson foundry and the foundry at the Memphis and Charleston Railroad converted their machinery to casting cannon and manufacturing munitions.

Factories for military supplies other than weapons employed 1,300–1,500 workers. Many Northern factory workers left the city and were replaced by trained city residents, including women and girls. In May 1861, up-river traffic was embargoed and boats were searched and detained. The riverfront was barricaded with a wall of cotton bales and the city council appropriated $59,000 for defense. However, travel on roads and railroads in and out of Memphis continued unhampered.

In the aftermath of Fort Sumter, Tennessee Governor Harris called for the immediate secession of Tennessee, declaring the "real Union" no longer existed. On May 6, the legislature drafted "A Declaration of Independence . . . Dissolving the Federal Relations between the State of Tennessee and the United States," which was submitted to the people for ratification in a June 8 vote. The declaration had a great deal of support in west and middle Tennessee, but east Tennesseans opposed its passage. Their opposition was in vain and Tennesseans approved the secession declaration and immediately joined the Confederate States of America. Shelby County voted 7,000–5 in favor of the referendum. A petition from east Tennesseans, who had voted more than 2–1 against secession, to allow them to separate from the state was rejected by a legislative committee.

In the first few months of the state's participation in the Confederacy, there was a holiday spirit in Memphis. It was tempered, though, by the greatest movement of people in and out of the city in its history to date. Northerners returned home to enlist in the Union Army or escape the scrutiny of their more militant Southern neighbors. Memphis became a hospital town when wounded Confederate soldiers were brought to the city after the battle of Belmont (Columbus). The initial jubilation gave way to growing indifference after Confederate losses in 1862 and as Memphis began to suffer from shortages of necessities, rising prices, and the loss of the cotton trade. Luxury items disappeared from store shelves; opera and theater performances no longer provided entertainment for citizens and visitors alike. What little cotton trickled into the city in the fall of 1861 was transferred for Confederate bonds offered in exchange for produce or specie. When capture of the city seemed imminent, cotton that had not been shipped out was burned.

General Braxton Bragg, Confederate commandant of the city, suspended municipal government in March 1862. Many Memphians fled the city after the fall of New Orleans in April and Corinth in early June. The withdrawal of Confederate troops from Fort Pillow and Randolph north of the city heightened concerns. On June 5, a Union fleet of 16 mortar boats, six rams (including the *Queen of the West*, *Monarch*, *Lancaster*, and *Switzerland*), eight iron clad gunboats,

Confederate sympathizers burned cotton to prevent it from falling into Union hands.

and a large number of tugs and transports, under the command of Army Colonel Charles Ellet, Jr., anchored just above Memphis. Three months earlier, U.S. Secretary of War Edwin M. Stanton had authorized Ellet to build a flotilla of steam rams for use against the Confederate Navy on the Mississippi and Ohio Rivers. Several of the rams were converted river towboats with heavily reinforced hulls for ramming and disabling enemy ships.

On June 6, 1862, nearly a year after Tennessee voted to join the Confederacy, Memphis fell to Union naval forces. The Battle of Memphis began before dawn and was over by 7:30 a.m. The Confederate River Defense Fleet, commanded by Commodore J.E. Montgomery, consisted of seven gunboats, six carrying two guns each, and the seventh carrying four guns. The Union fleet had a total of 84 guns to the Confederate's 16. From the bluffs, about 5,000 Memphians watched the battle take place in a river channel that was so narrow the boats had a difficult time maneuvering. The fighting consisted mainly of vessels ramming each other. The Union's technological advantage was enhanced by the fact that their powerful vessels were moving downstream. Skillful maneuvering by the *Monarch* resulted in a head-on collision between two Confederate ships, the *General Beauregard* and the *General Price*. Ellet was mortally wounded during a fight between his ship, the *Queen of the West*, and two Confederate rams, and died 15 days later. But by the end of the Battle of Memphis, all but one Confederate boat that had been held in reserve was sunk or disabled. Ellet's son, Charles Rivers Ellet, took a party of sailors and marched to the post office on the corner of Third and Jefferson Streets and raised the American flag on the rooftop. An angry crowd taunted the flag party and locked them on the rooftop, but the only shooting came from an insurance agent named Crook who fired a pistol at the group from the crowd below. The Union gunboat commander, Charles Henry Davis, threatened to shell the city and Ellet and his men were finally released. Mayor John Park surrendered the city to Davis. The 43rd and 46th Indiana Regiments landed later in the day and raised another flag at the corner of Jefferson and Front.

The Union Army constructed Fort Pickering at the site of the federal fort abandoned in the early 1800s. The 2-mile long fortification stretched from the bluffs below Beale Avenue to the Indian mounds at what is now DeSoto Park. Six thousand slaves and free blacks, who came into the city after its fall, were eventually pressed into service constructing the fort. At first, the Northern merchants who rushed to the city after June 1862 were unable to stimulate trade and commerce. Stores in the city remained closed despite a proclamation ordering that they open. But U.S. Treasury agents arrived in the city soon after its fall and a board of trade was organized. Within weeks, Memphis was open for business.

Memphis' most important wartime role, whether under Confederate or Union control, was as a center for trade and commerce. Even after its capture by the Union, goods continued to flow from the city to Southern soldiers and Confederate sympathizers in the countryside. As historian Gerald Capers noted, "The Confederate army may have been fed from the granaries of Georgia and

Union Army Colonel Charles Ellet's fleet of steam-powered rams defeated the Confederate River Defense Fleet in the Battle of Memphis.

Alabama, but its martial necessaries were smuggled through the lines from the cities of the upper West no less than from the Bahamas."[18] Southerners smuggled medicine out of the city in funeral carriages or hid gold in the stomachs of dead animals that were then carried to a dump heap beyond Union lines. Women smuggled contraband items out of the city in their clothing or sent their slaves into the city to purchase restricted goods, which were sent on to friends and relatives in the Confederate Army. Between June 1862 and June 1864, $20–30 million worth of supplies reached the Confederacy through Memphis. The succession of Union generals put in charge of the city—Ulysses S. Grant, William T. Sherman, S.A. Hurlburt, and C.C. Washburn—all tried to minimize the smuggling, but with mixed results.

The most significant development in Civil War Memphis was the migration of African Americans into the city. Between 1862 and 1865, thousands of blacks fled mid-South plantations and farms for camps and shantytowns in and around Corinth, Mississippi, and Memphis and LaGrange, Tennessee. Escaping slaves were drawn to Memphis by the presence of the Union Army and civilian agencies as well as aid societies like the American Missionary Association. African-American migrants were also attracted by opportunities to establish or reunite families and to construct new identities as free men and women. By 1865, a seemingly endless surge of men, women, and children from the rural Mississippi Delta changed the composition and the character of African-American life in Memphis. For the first time in its history, a significant proportion of the city's population was black.

Union policies concerning escaping slaves were confusing and contradictory in the first years of the war. Army officials in Memphis, as in other parts of the South, thought of the Civil War as a "white man's war" that would have little effect on the status of slavery. Military officials at first refused to harbor escaping slaves. General Order Number 19, issued two days after the city surrendered,

Alexander Simplot's sketch shows Union sailors raising the American flag over the post office after their victory in the 90-minute Battle of Memphis.

excluded all African Americans "except those who came with the command to this place" from the Union's lines. The order was designed to discourage fugitives from entering the city and prevent escapes by riverboat; however, a few months later as the goal of the war changed from one of preserving the federal union to emancipating slaves, General Order Number 19 was replaced with General Order Number 72, which prohibited the army from returning fugitive slaves to their owners. Instead, they were treated as "contraband" of war, allowed behind Union lines, and put to work building fortifications or working as support personnel (cooks, washerwomen, servants) for Union soldiers.

General Ulysses S. Grant appointed Captain John Eaton as Superintendent of Freedmen for the Mississippi Valley. One of Eaton's major responsibilities was establishing special quarters for fugitives and refugees. In March 1863, Tennessee camps were consolidated and residents sent to the three sites near Memphis—Camps Fiske and Shiloh near Fort Pickering, and Camp Dixie on Presidents Island. A year later, residents of the Corinth, Mississippi camp were sent to Camp Dixie. The camps were sometimes portrayed in almost idyllic terms by Northern missionary teachers like Lucinda Humphrey:

> The contraband camps at the post of Memphis, three in No., are beautifully located. A deep ravine south of the city separates the fort from Camp Shiloh, and another ravine just below separates Shiloh from Camp Fiske. These are on a high bluff overlooking the Mississippi and opposite—a little south of this camp is camp Dixie on the President's island. Shiloh is a village of log houses and camp Fiske consists of three

long rows of cabins, numbering 109, besides quarters for whites, and the large church and school house. The camp on the island at present consists of tents. [19]

However, the constant movement of freed people through the camps made it difficult to organize camp life. Many arrived during the "sickly season [winter]" with little clothing, few cooking utensils, and already in poor health. By the summer of 1863, over 1,000 people were housed in the tents at the President's Island camp. Conditions deteriorated even further when an additional 1,500 freed people were relocated from Corinth to the Presidents Island late in the winter of 1863–1864. In January–February 1865, over 100 people died, including the camp commandant. One observer noted "on the evening before last there were five [contraband] came into our camp from Mississippi all of whom were more or less frostbitten. Some of their feet were so badly frozen that amputation will be necessary."[20]

In 1864, more than 7,000 black men enlisted and trained in the Memphis area, almost a third of African-American enlistees in the state as a whole. Many were recruited from the contraband camps. Black soldiers fought at the battle of Moscow, Tennessee, in December 1863 and at Brice's Crossroads and Tupelo, Mississippi. They were also part of the garrison at Fort Pillow who refused to surrender when Confederate forces, under the command of Nathan Bedford Forrest, attacked in April 1864. Confederate troops routed Union soldiers sent to reinforce the Fort Pillow garrison and stormed the fort. The resulting "massacre" became a rallying cry for African-American soldiers.

The Union Army recruited African-American men, like the one pictured in this photograph, from contraband camps in the city for service in the United States Colored Troops. By the end of the war, about 20,000 black soldiers were recruited into the Union Army from Tennessee.

The migration of over 15,000 African Americans into Memphis was countered by the departure of thousands of Confederate sympathizers. By early 1863, the city's population included only 11,000 of the original white inhabitants, 5,000 slaves, and 19,000 newcomers. Many military-age white men left to join the Confederate Army. Some merchants also fled, creating an immediate problem in the aftermath of the Battle of Memphis of reestablishing the economic sector. The arrival of Northern businessmen eventually solved this problem. But the reopened trade went north and south out of the city. Despite Union occupation, Memphis remained a center for illicit trade to the Confederate forces throughout the Civil War.

Although white Memphians resented the loyalty oaths, the military pass system, and constant changes in regulations, these restrictions also fell heavily on the city's black population. In July 1863, General Order Number 75 required all free blacks and mulattoes living in Memphis to find some "responsible white person" to work for or go to the contraband camps under the supervision of the Freedman's Bureau. Black Memphians, long-time residents and newcomers alike, protested that they could "not be free, if a white man has to have his name on their passes" and criticized the indiscriminate roundups of African Americans for pass violations. White Memphians countered that the order had the "wholesome effect in stirring the negroes to a realization of the responsibility resting upon them in their new relation."[21] The purpose of the order, according to one local newspaper, was to protect Memphians "from the tax of supporting a large number of contraband [by] inducing the negro to return to his master, or go to the contraband camps where order, discipline and work will be executed."[22]

In October 1863, military officials replaced General Order Number 75 with Order Number 42, revoking all passes issued between July and October and requiring employers to certify that those for whom they requested passes were actually working for them. Employers were also responsible for the behavior of their employees. The army issued the new order to thwart the growing business of fraudulent passes marketed to anxious African Americans who could not find legitimate employers. One official later noted that "both white and colored citizens gave passes to nearly every Negro that asked for them. In some cases it was converted into a regular business and the sum of one or two dollars was given to obtain these certificates."

In addition to their concern about the smuggling of goods out of the city, Union officials were also concerned by open displays of loyalty from white Confederate sympathizers. Guards were ordered to shoot anyone who disrespected the American flag. Some, like Elizabeth Avery Meriwether, whose husband Minor was serving with the Confederate Army in Mississippi, were ordered out of the city. Others were sent to Irving Block, the "Bastille of the South," located on the north side of Court Square. In 1864, Mayor John Park was imprisoned in Irving Block for suspected disloyalty and the city government was dissolved.

General Nathan Bedford Forrest led 3,000 men in an attack on Memphis.

Yet civilians who sympathized with the Confederacy posed less of a problem for Federal troops than the exploits of Confederate General Nathan Bedford Forrest, whose 5,000 troops waged guerrilla warfare from their camps just south of the Tennessee border in northern Mississippi. In early August 1864, the Union command in Memphis sent 18,000 troops into Mississippi to suppress the Confederate attacks. Forrest retaliated by leading 3,000 of his men in an assault on Memphis. The purpose of the attack was three-fold: to capture the three Union generals posted in Memphis, to release Confederate prisoners from Irving Block, and to force the Union troops who were closing in on the Confederate camp in Mississippi back to defend Memphis. Two of the Union generals, though, were not at home at the time of the attack and the third, General Washburn, abandoned his wife and his dress uniform to escape down a nearby alley in his nightshirt. The attack on Irving Block was also unsuccessful. However, Forrest's raid did force the Union Army to return to Memphis to protect their economic and military interests in the city.

The Confederate surrender to the Union at Appomattox in 1865 brought an end to four years of bloody conflict. Up and down the Mississippi River soldiers mustered out of both armies and headed back to their homes, yet wartime tragedies continued to plague Memphis. In the early morning hours of April 26, 1865, the steamer *Sultana* left the city's wharves. More than 2,000 passengers were aboard the two-year-old side-wheeler—six times the vessel's capacity. Most were Union soldiers recently mustered out or freed from Confederate prison camps. The *Sultana* had experienced problems with leaky boilers since leaving New Orleans five days earlier. Repair crews at Vicksburg and Memphis thought they

By the end of the Civil War, the African-American population in Memphis had quadrupled to nearly 16,000 or 39 percent of the city's total population.

had solved the problems, but explosions rocked the steamer as she rounded a bend in the Mississippi River near a cluster of islands called "Hens and Chickens." Passengers, crew, and cargo were thrown into the river's icy waters. Men grabbed anything that would float. Hot coals ignited the wooden vessel; the *Sultana*'s twin smokestacks toppled into the river, pinning victims underneath. The rescue boats that left Memphis as soon as they heard the explosions pulled victims and survivors from the water and both shores all the way from the city to the spot near Marion, Arkansas, where the *Sultana* finally sank. Years of physical deprivations in Southern prison camps doomed many of the passengers to watery graves. The exact number of casualties of the *Sultana* tragedy will never be known because Union authorities had not made out muster rolls when the men boarded at Vicksburg, but most estimates place the figure between 1,700 and 1,800 (almost 300 more perished than when the Titanic sank in 1912 after striking an iceberg in the Atlantic Ocean).

Memphis experienced another catastrophe one year later when a violent racial confrontation rocked the city. The growing number of African-American migrants, who arrived in the city during the war, posed problems for civil and military officials. Newspapers carried almost daily accounts attributing rising crime rates to the newcomers from the rural countryside. Inadequate housing and a shortage of jobs made life in the city even more difficult, especially as the Freedman's Bureau reduced its services in the late 1860s. Rations were cut off in the fall of 1865, the Freedman's Hospital was broken up, and the Bureau ordered all black orphans to be apprenticed. City and county authorities initially refused to assume responsibility for care of indigent or destitute freedpeople; when they did provide assistance, it was rarely adequate. An organization of prominent freedmen, the Freedmen's Sanitary Commission and Hospital Fund, was authorized by the Freedmen's Bureau to collect a tax of $1 from freedpeople to provide social services for the community.

Missionary workers, military officials, and Freedmen's Bureau agents felt that returning to the fields was the only recourse for the "surplus" of freedpeople in the city. One agent noted that:

> There is an abundant demand for labor in this district . . .[the Bureau and the military should] take efficient steps to remove the portion of the Freedpeople about this city, who have no legitimate means of support and distribute them in the Country, where their labor is wanted and where they will have much better opportunities of leading useful and happy lives.[23]

In the rural countryside, a woman could earn $10–18 a month in the fields while men earned $15–25, and employers provided each family with a house. However, many African Americans, perhaps aware of the physical violence and economic exploitation of freedpeople in the countryside, resisted efforts to expel them from the city.

Many blacks who chose to remain in the city congregated in an area around Beale, Linden, Turley, St. Martin, and Causey Streets referred to as the "Negro Quarters" by some white Memphians. African Americans who had lived in the city before the Civil War (as free blacks or as slaves) and newcomers opened boarding houses, hotels, groceries, and other retail establishments in the community. Black churches, schools, and other community institutions also developed during and after the war. Memphis was also dealing with an Irish immigrant population clustered in these same neighborhoods. Although the two groups competed for space and influence in postwar Memphis, they sometimes shared dwellings in crowded, unsanitary tenements like those at numbers 99, 101, and 103 Causey Street where 50 to 75 black and white people occupied a building with no privies, not even in the yard. This proximity sometimes bred conflict and violence both within households and between ethnic groups.

The mustering out and disarming of the Third U.S. Colored Heavy Artillery in late April 1866 was the catalyst for the Memphis Riot. The violence began with a struggle between four Memphis policemen and three or four African-American soldiers on the afternoon of Monday, April 30. Witnesses later testified that the police officers encountered the soldiers on Causey Street. The groups exchanged words. As the black men moved to let the policemen pass by one man fell and a policeman tripped over him. The other lawmen drew their pistols and knives and when the man who had fallen started to leave, they ran after him. A fight ensued between the soldiers and the police before the two groups parted.

This was the prelude to a three-day assault on black residents and their property in the South Memphis neighborhood of the city's Sixth and Seventh Wards. The violent rampage began on the afternoon of May 1 and lasted until May 3. Forty-six African Americans were reportedly killed, but many assaults and deaths probably went unreported as terrified blacks left the city during and after the riot. Only two whites were killed. Seventy-five people were wounded, five black women were raped, one hundred robberies occurred, and one hundred and seven homes, churches, businesses, and schools were destroyed. White teachers in the Freedmen's Bureau and missionary schools left the city because of threats to their safety, but these fears were short lived. Instructors returned, schools were rebuilt, and black and white Memphis returned to an uneasy normalcy during the Reconstruction Period.

Forty-six blacks and two whites were killed, hundreds of blacks were beaten and robbed, five women were raped, and homes, churches and schoolhouses were destroyed in three days of racial violence in May 1866.

6. Yellow Fever and the Taxing District

The transition to peace was easier in Memphis than in other Southern cities because it escaped physical and economic destruction during the war. Trade had continued almost uninterrupted from the city's wharves. Union military and civilian personnel (as well as Confederate sympathizers) flocked to Memphis' stores and markets. Many businesses not only survived but prospered as Union merchants and artisans replaced Confederates who left the city after June 1862. By 1865, the value of taxable property in the city was about the same as it had been in 1860. Commercial activity recovered quickly and whatever transportation (river and railroad) had been interrupted was soon restored. The city also experienced dramatic population increases during and after the war. By early 1866, over 1,000 houses were under construction, a street railway company was operating in some areas, and 90 workers ran 5,000 spindles at cotton mills along the Wolf River.

Memphis still depended on the cotton from farms and plantations in western Tennessee and northern Mississippi for its livelihood and the Chamber of Commerce organized a subscription drive to reconstruct the Mississippi and Tennessee Railroad so crops could be transported to downtown wharves. Local foundries also returned to production and turned out agricultural equipment to help redevelop the rural hinterland. However, in the years immediately following the war, the mid-South farmers faced a series of critical problems: an 1865 federal tax on all Southern cotton (which was lifted in 1866), short cotton crops and famine in 1867, limited capital for investment coupled with bank failures and economic stagnation in 1868, and shortages of white laborers. In 1869, a Convention on Immigration convened to discuss how to encourage European immigration to the city, but the demand for black labor was more limited. City leaders and federal officials felt the main occupation for Southern black workers must continue to be on the cotton farms and plantations of western Tennessee and northern Mississippi. Most blacks men could only find work in heavy manual labor on the wharves, at railroad depots, in warehouses, and in the cottonseed mills; for women, it was as washers and ironers or domestic laborers.

Although the Custom House and Post Office is a prominent feature in this photograph of Memphis, the cotton stacked on the levee waiting for transport dominated the city's economy.

In 1878, the hot, muggy atmosphere of late summer brought a disaster to Memphis rivaling the wartime chaos of the previous decade. In mid-July, reports reached the city of outbreaks of yellow fever in New Orleans. For the next month, the disease moved ominously upriver. In each of the two previous decades, the disease had attacked the city. In 1855, about 220 residents succumbed to the illness, which claimed another 595 victims 12 years later. In 1873, a combination of cholera, smallpox, and yellow fever claimed 2,000 victims. Although the cause of the fever was unknown in the 1870s, many people assumed there was some connection to the filth and poor sanitation common in nineteenth-century cities. In the 1840s, Dr. Carlos Finlay had suggested insects might be the carriers of yellow fever, but when the disease struck Memphis in 1878, the world was still two decades away from Dr. Walter Reed's successful eradication of yellow fever in Cuba. In 1870s Memphis, stagnant water in bayous and upturned receptacles, as well as noxious gases from garbage and dead animals, seemed the most likely sources of disease. Few people connected the deadly plague to the tiny insects that were part and parcel of a summer evening in the river city.

When reports of yellow fever in New Orleans reached Memphis, the city quarantined boats on the river, sprinkled lime in the streets, and fired cannons to dispel "miasma" in the air. In spite of these feeble efforts, the first cases were detected in mid-July. Hundreds of Memphians fled the city even before the official announcement of an epidemic was issued on August 13. Within four days, another 25,000 left Memphis, spreading the disease to outlying communities. Neighboring towns imposed their own quarantines to try and contain the epidemic, but with little success. Years later, activist Ida B. Wells would write of the 1878 epidemic's deadly assault on her hometown of Holly Springs, Mississippi. Wells' father, mother, and young brother died from the disease and young Ida Wells became the sole support of her other siblings. Thousands of Memphis residents who were unwilling to stay in the city but unable to entirely escape the area lived in refugee camps on the city's outskirts.

Although some residents assumed that African Americans had a natural immunity to yellow fever, black and white Memphians were stricken. Fourteen thousand African Americans and 6,000 whites remained in the city during the epidemic. More blacks than whites probably stayed because they had fewer resources enabling them to leave. Of the blacks who remained, 11,000 were eventually stricken and 949 died. Among these victims was one of the city's first African-American schoolteachers, Graphtil Moody. If, as many observers noted, having someone to care for the victim gave them a better chance of survival, the fact that more blacks remained in the city probably enhanced the survival chances for African-American victims. Almost all of the 6,000 whites who remained in the city contracted yellow fever, and over 4,000 died.

The Howard Association, which was first organized in New Orleans in 1853 and brought to Memphis during the 1855 yellow fever outbreak, provided physicians, nurses, supplies, and assistance during the epidemic. The Association's membership doubled from 15 to 32 during the scourge. The group, made of men from ordinary jobs, collected and dispensed more than $500,000 in assistance, and hired 2,900 nurses and 11 doctors. The Howards also organized burial details. Nineteen of its members were eventually stricken and ten died, including the president, Butler P. Anderson. Dr. R.H. Tate, the first African-American doctor to practice in the city, came from Cincinnati to aid the Howard Association. He was assigned to the area west of Lauderdale and south of Union,

Harper's Weekly sketches show Memphis during the yellow fever epidemic.

better known as "Hell's Half Acre." Tate and three other Ohio doctors eventually succumbed to yellow fever.

The nuns from St. Mary's Episcopal Cathedral turned their residence into an infirmary and dispensary. They also cared for orphans, including many whose parents died in the epidemic, at the Church Home Orphanage and at the Canfield Asylum, which had been established in 1865 as a home for African-American orphans. Four of the nuns, Sisters Constance, Thecla, Ruth, and Frances, died, as did Reverends Charles Parsons and Louis Schuyler. At the other end of the social spectrum, two local madams, Emily Sutton and Annie Cook, sent their girls away and turned their houses into hospitals. Cook died three weeks after she began nursing the sick. African Americans nursed the sick, buried the dead, and a black militia unit patrolled the city streets to keep order.

By the time the epidemic ended with the first frost in mid-October, many Memphians had abandoned the city; and others followed in the aftermath of another yellow fever crisis the following year. The Reconstruction-era debt crisis that had plagued Memphis for decades was exacerbated by the lost of a substantial portion of the city's population and tax base. In 1874, some Memphians called for city leaders to renounce the city charter to avoid payment of over $5 million in debt believed to be unethical and illegally contracted—the city was bankrupt. In January 1879, after the state repealed its charter, Memphis ceased to exist as a corporate entity and became a taxing district. Municipal affairs were placed under the control of two commissions, a three-member Board of Fire and Police, and a five-member Board of Public Works. Commissioners served two-year terms. Presidents of the Fire and Police Commission included David T. Porter, John Overton, Jr., David Park Hadden, William D. Bethell, and Walker Lucas Clapp. Half of these eight commissioners were initially appointed by the governor; eventually all were elected. Holders of city bonds challenged the creation of the taxing district, but lost their case in the United States Supreme Court. Under the Taxing District, Memphis "instituted sanitary measures to prevent a recurrence of yellow fever and then negotiated a settlement of the city's debt."[24] A public sewer system was developed, strict sanitary ordinances were instituted, and regular garbage collection was inaugurated in the city. Decaying wood pavement was replaced with limestone and gravel surfaces. The city returned to home rule in 1893.

African Americans were active in the city's political life from the 1870s through the 1890s. Two men, Alexander H. Dickerson and H.E. Pinn, were on the Board of Common Councilmen in 1872; four in 1873 (Turner Hunt, Thomas Mason, Edward Shaw, and Joseph Clouston, Jr.), and six in 1874 (Clouston, Hunt, Jacob H. Moon, George E. Page, James Thomas, and James D. Walters). Thomas presided over the Council for at least one day in 1874 and Shaw was also appointed wharf master the same year. Clouston and Moon were reelected to their third and second terms the following year. From 1876 until the creation of the Taxing District in 1879, one or two African Americans always served on the Council.

Governmental reorganization under the Taxing District diluted the political influence of African Americans in the city and no blacks served on the commissions until 1882 when Lymus Wallace was elected to the Board of Public Works. Wallace was elected to a second four-year term in 1886. He was the last African American elected to the city council for 78 years.

Two African Americans, Fred Savage and Alfred Froman, served on the school board in the late nineteenth century, and Josiah Settle was assistant attorney general of the Criminal Court. Isham F. Norris and Thomas Frank Cassels represented Memphis and Shelby Council in the Tennessee General Assembly from 1881–1883. Norris represented the city and county again from 1891to 1893. African Americans also served on the city's police force from the 1870s to the 1890s, although the last black policeman, Dallas Lee, retired in 1895. Lee was an officer for 17 years, walking a beat as a uniformed policeman, working as a special detective, and driving a patrol wagon.

Lymus Wallace served as a city alderman from 1882–1890.

7. The Mistress of the Valley

On May 12, 1892, 50,000 people lined the Chickasaw Bluff for the opening of the Great Mississippi River Bridge. The 8,000-foot crossing was the longest span in the United States and the third longest in the world. Built by the Kansas City, Fort Scott and Memphis Railroad, the "Frisco Bridge," as it would later be called, was the first bridge across the Mississippi River below St. Louis. Memphians celebrated the opening with two days of parades, banquets, speeches, and spectacles. Visitors could also ride the city's first elevator to the roof of the *Memphis Daily Appeal* building to get a view of the city and bridge. A caravan of 18 locomotives, each covered with garlands of flowers, were linked together to make the first trip across the river. Engineers and firemen volunteered for this run, but at the last minute one fireman backed out and was replaced by a shop boy. The courageous crews were showered with kisses from a bevy of pretty girls and cannons boomed as the caravan inched toward the river. The crowd waited breathlessly as the locomotives moved across the bridge to Arkansas. They were greeted by more cannon fire, riverboat whistles, bells, and cheers when they arrived safely on the other side.

The opening of the Great River Bridge symbolized Memphis' emergence as a New South city. The population, nearly double the post-Yellow Fever epidemic figure, now totaled 64,495, and would pass 100,000 by 1900. The 1890 annexation of several tracts of land extended the city's boundaries to McLemore on the south, Elmwood, Belleview, Waldran, and Brinkley Avenues on the east, and Vollentine and the Wolf River on the north. City neighborhoods and business districts were linked to suburban areas by 65 miles of street railroads. The first street railway system, developed in 1866, initially consisted of mule-drawn streetcars. An electric streetcar was introduced in 1891 and a trolley system during the same decade. The expanded Citizen's Street Railway, created in a merger with the Memphis City Railroad Company, boasted 60 motor cars and 100 trailers. Its rails were laid along the city's principal streets and passed all the major hotels and businesses. The railway also ran through the major residential areas and to suburban resorts. In 1900, the Memphis Street Railway Company was established. It had 100 miles of track and 75 cars. Other railway companies serviced residential districts east of the Montgomery Park race track and fair grounds and around the Magnolia Park area. The Raleigh Springs Railroad carried passengers to the summer resort at the Springs, about 9 miles from the city.

The paving of streets with asphalt also improved transportation in the city, and Samuel T. Carnes brought electricity and telephone service to the city. Carnes received the franchise for the Bell system in the 1870s and made the city's first call in 1877. He sold his telephone service to a Nashville company in 1883. About the same time, Carnes secured rights for an electric-light service and began to offer commercial service soon after he sold his telephone company. Until this time, lighting in the city was provided by the Memphis Gas Light Company, which had been organized in 1851. Private customers paid $1.75 per 1,000 cubic feet for light and $1.50 per 1,000 cubic feet for fuel and power. The company also furnished the city gas for 600 street lamps and service to city buildings. The Memphis Light and Power Company was organized in 1890, when Carnes merged his company with a competitor. The new business received a ten-year charter from the city to provide local service and monopolized electrical service in the city for the next 20 years.

Improvements in the city's water supply, street paving, and a new sewer system all made Memphis a safer and more attractive place to live and work. Although population increased dramatically in the 1880s, there were 423 fewer deaths in 1890 than in 1884. In 1880, 1 mile of sewers with 100 connections had been completed; 12 years later, the city boasted 63 miles of sewers with 10,000

In 1892, 50,000 people gathered on the bluffs to watch the opening of the Great Mississippi River Bridge.

connections. For much of the nineteenth century, drinking water and water for fire companies was drawn from the Wolf River. The city's first water works, the Memphis Water Company, was organized in 1873. The discovery of a huge reservoir of underground water provided Memphians with an unlimited supply of the cleanest, best-tasting water in the region. By 1887, companies were pumping water from 40 artesian wells sunk to a depth of 400–500 feet into sand beneath the city. Five years later, 6,000 customers used 10 million gallons of water from the wells. About 25,000 tons of ice were also produced. More wells were sunk along and adjacent to the Gayoso bayou and the Louisville and Nashville Railroad. The capacity of the system could be expanded as the city's needs grew. The city government purchased the water companies in 1903 and water rates were reduced by 20 percent the following year.

The artesian well system also benefited the city's only brewery, Tennessee Brewing Company, located at the corner of Butler and Tennessee Streets. The brewery produced 200,000 barrels of beer marketed under its principal brands, Pilsener, Export, and Budweiser. Built in 1885, the brewery had its own artesian wells and made about 35 tons of ice daily. The brewery also operated its own stables, cooperage, and bottling works.

By the 1890s, downtown Memphis was a thriving business and entertainment area. The majestic Federal Building and the Cossitt Library (opened in 1893) dominated the riverfront. The library was named for successful Memphis merchant and Northern businessman Frederick H. Cossitt, whose heirs donated $75,000 to establish Memphis' first public library. Further back were the 11-story Continental Bank (D.T. Porter) Building (built in 1895), the new Gayoso House, the Peabody Hotel, the Grand Opera House, and the Lyceum. Majestic churches dotted the city's landscape, testimony to the continuing influence of religion in a city with a solid reputation as a raucous river town. First Methodist Church, which dated back to the city's first decades, was rebuilt on North Second Street in 1887. The granite building was designed by Jacob Snyder of Ohio in the "Akron plan" of locating the Sunday School rooms at the rear of the sanctuary. Neighboring First Presbyterian Church also opened a new building in 1884 after the roof of the original structure collapsed in 1873 and a fire destroyed the building in 1883.

In 1871, the congregation of First Baptist Beale Street laid the cornerstone for the first stone church built by African Americans in the South. The two-story building housed Sunday School classes and offices on the first floor, with the entire second floor devoted to the auditorium. An immersion baptistery was located in the front and gallery on each side and in the back of the auditorium. And while the righteous found their seats in church the rowdy might wake up in the nearby commodious Shelby County Jail. By 1892, Memphis had more banks than any Southern city of comparable size except for New Orleans. There were nine commercial banks with a surplus capital of $6,554,000 and deposits of $8,130,000, and seven savings banks with capital and surplus of $525,000 and deposits of $1,480,000. Local insurance companies also had capital valued at over $1 million.

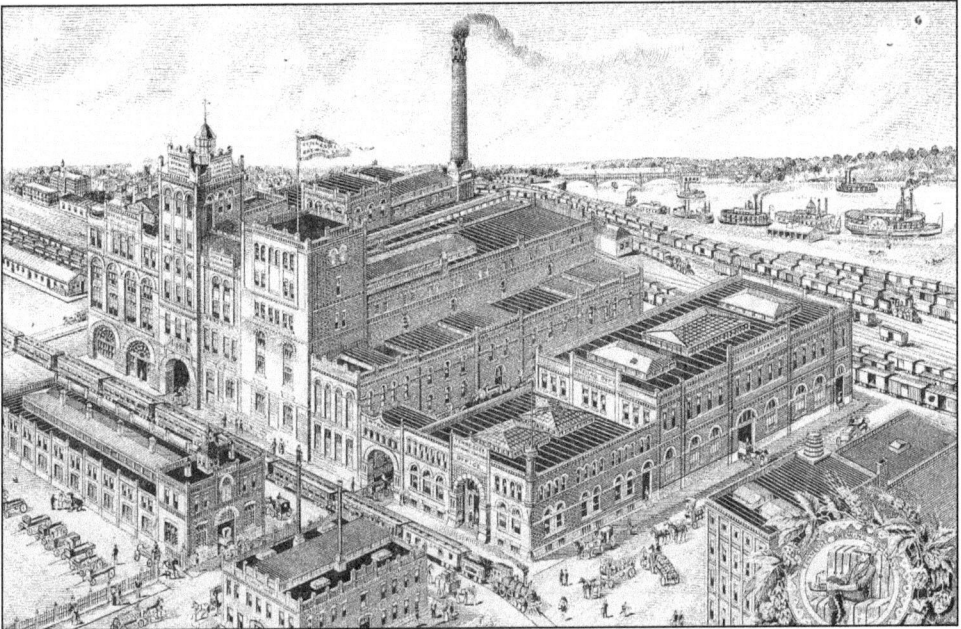

This view shows the Artesian Water Company in 1899. By the end of the nineteenth century, about 10 million gallons of water were pumped from artesian wells drilled in the sandy soil beneath the city.

Financial barons like Napoleon Hill (the "merchant prince of Memphis") and George Arnold represented a new generation of Memphis capitalists who made their fortunes from innovations in transportation and communication as well as the mainstay of Memphis' nineteenth century economy, the cotton industry. Hill and Arnold were organizers, promoters, and executives of the Citizen's Street Railway Company as well as stockholders in the city's banks and insurance companies. Hill was also involved in cotton warehousing and real estate. Bavarian immigrant Louis Hanauer arrived in Memphis after the Civil War, established a wholesale grocery and cotton factor house, and made his fortune in the city's insurance companies, the German National Bank, Hanauer Oil Works, National Cotton-seed Oil, and Huller Company, and Star Oil Mills. Elias Lowenstein, a German immigrant who came to Memphis in 1854, became a wholesale and retail dealer in dry goods. Like the city's other economic leaders, Lowenstein was also involved in banking and cotton factoring.

The lumber industry gained ground in Memphis between 1880 and 1900. When the Great Mississippi River Bridge opened in 1892, there were 250 saw mills within a 150-mile radius of Memphis. The bridge provided lumber merchants a more direct link to the Pacific coast and to foreign markets. Capitalization in the lumber industry grew from $200,000 in 1880 to $2.5 million by 1900. That year Memphis was the world's largest hardwood market and the world's second largest overall lumber market. Barrels, boxes, doors, blinds, and

69

This elaborate house was home of Napoleon Hill, the "merchant prince of Memphis," whose business interest included the presidency of the Chamber of Commerce, Cotton Exchange, the Union and Planter's Bank, and the Citizen's Street Railway Company.

wagons were manufactured in Memphis and, in 1893, the Memphis Furniture Manufacturing Company opened its doors.

A small number of other industries developed in late nineteenth century Memphis. Manogue Iron Company and Pidgeon-Thomas Iron Works produced iron and steel products and True-Tagg Paint Company, which opened in 1896, produced paint for the region. Broom factories, mattress makers, blacksmiths, and slaughter houses also emerged during this period. Memphis was home to the largest boot and shoe market in the South and one of the largest wholesale grocery markets in the nation. The city also boasted trade in livestock, especially mules; by the early 1900s, it was the largest mule market in the world. However, despite all indications of financial diversity in Memphis, cotton and the river continued to dominate the city's landscape and its economic life.

In 1891–1892, 770,000 bales of cotton were shipped from Memphis. This was almost twice the number from ten years earlier and the city remained the largest inland cotton market in the country. The cotton trade was growing because of the city's facilities for marketing, financing, selling, and transporting cotton. Twelve cotton compresses handled 15,000 bales a day and the city had storage capacity for 300,000 bales. Memphians engaged in every branch of the cotton trade from the factors, bankers, and grocers (who provided farmers with resources and financing, marketed the cotton crops, and collected commissions on crop sales) to cotton classers, clerks, compress hands, float drivers, and laborers. Many of the large cotton commission houses were located at "Cotton Row" on Front Street between Jefferson and Beale. Among the city's leading cotton factors, merchandisers, and grocers were Howell Cotton Company, which handled about 250,000 bales per year; Townsend, Cowie and Company of Liverpool, England, which handled over 45,000 bales; Watson, Wood & Company of Liverpool, England; W.F. Taylor & Company; J.T. Fargason & Company; and Fly & Hobson. The five-story Cotton Exchange Building housed the Memphis Cotton Exchange (organized in 1873), as well as the offices of the Merchants, Lumber, and Real Estate Exchanges; Western Union; the Telegraph Company; the Government Signal Office; and the Weather Bureau.

By 1890, African Americans made up 44 percent of Memphis' population. Black men made up nearly 33 percent of the city's male labor force, while black women made up more than 75 percent of the female labor force. Most black men worked as laborers or in the city's cotton-related industries, while black women worked as cooks and domestic servants, midwives, nurses, and laundresses. Some working class black women lived in the households of their white employers; others occupied small shanties in the alleys near more prosperous white households. Many others worked outside their homes, but did not live in or near their employers' households. Instead, they depended on the street railways for transportation to their jobs.

African Americans lived throughout the city, yet black neighborhoods that began developing in the suburbs of the city in the post–Civil War period spread outward by the late nineteenth century. In the Klondyke area of northeast Memphis, African American's owned nearly 95 percent of the land and black landowners also controlled much of the land in New Chicago. Black neighborhoods developed along South Lauderdale, South Parkway East, St. Paul, South Orleans, East Dudley, and Linden. Black Memphis was divided along social class lines with the families of black physicians, dentists, lawyers, businessmen, and other professionals cultivating "a refined and graceful colored society which they maintained by rigid discrimination favoring only the educated, light-complexioned, and well mannered." The small black elite included families like the Robert R. Churches and Josiah Settles, who maintained personal, political, social, and economic relationships with "aristocrats of color" in other parts of the country and influenced the political, economic, and social life of black Memphis. Much of this influence was in racially segregated schools, churches, and community-based small businesses.

By the end of the nineteenth century, Memphis was a city divided into clearly identifiable black and white neighborhoods with segregated hospitals, schools, churches, hotels, restaurants, and cemeteries. Poll taxes, instituted in Tennessee in the 1890s, did not completely disfranchise African-American men in Memphis, but as the century closed their choices were limited to white candidates. Lymus Wallace was the last African American to serve in city government until the 1960s; and no African Americans were elected to the school board from the 1880s until the 1960s.

In the 1890s, racial violence peaked and, while lynchings occurred across the state, western Tennessee seemed to have more than its share. Between 1882 and 1900, 11 men died at the hands of lynch mobs in Memphis and Shelby County. In 1892, the relative calm of race relations in Memphis was shattered by the brutal lynchings of Calvin McDowell, Will Stewart, and Tom Moss. The three owned a joint stock company, the People's Grocery Store, in a predominantly black neighborhood. Competition with a neighboring white grocer led to a confrontation between the black businessmen and what they thought was a white mob. McDowell, Stewart, and Moss were arrested, but were taken from the jail four days later and shot to death. Ida B. Wells, editor of the *Free Speech*, used her newspaper to encourage blacks to boycott Memphis' streetcars and even leave the city. Wells wrote stinging indictments of white lynch mobs challenging the argument that black men were lynched for raping white women.

> Eight negroes lynched since last issue of the Free Speech. Three were charged with killing white men and five with raping white women. Nobody in this section believes the old thread-bare lie that Negro men assault white women. If Southern white men are not careful they will over-reach themselves and a conclusion will be reached which will be very damaging to the moral reputation of their women.[25]

Weeks later, Wells was out of the city when her newspaper office was destroyed and the business manager run out of town. She moved to New York, published anti-lynching articles in T. Thomas Fortune's *New York Age* and joined forces with African-American club women and the international anti-lynching movement to challenge mob violence in the South.

In July 1893, Lee Walker was charged with assaulting a white woman, Mollie McCadden, and dragged from his cell in the Shelby County jail by a drunken mob of about 1,000 men. According to one observer, the mob, "howling like savages and licking their chops like hungry Numidian lions," tore off Walker's clothes, cut his throat, and hung him from a telephone pole two blocks from the downtown jail. The body was later cut down and burned and the remains left at the front of the court house to serve as "a hideous memento of [the mob's] contempt of Law." Local newspapers denounced the sheriff and deputies as cowards for surrendering their prisoner without a fight, but the greatest concern was the impact the lynching would have on the city's image. The sheriff and deputies were indicted by a Grand Jury, but prosecutors were unable to proceed with a trial because, out of 100 men summoned for jury duty, only one man could be found who was competent to serve.

A year later, in a third episode of racial violence, six black prisoners were murdered on their way to Memphis from Kerrville in northern Shelby County. The men had been arrested for barn-burning by a Memphis detective who was bringing them back to the city by wagon when they were waylaid by a mob near Big Creek. The apprehension and trial of the "Big Creek" lynchers, which was covered extensively in the local, state and national, further tarnished the image of Memphis as a progressive, New South city. The jury was impaneled from citizens of the city and eastern Shelby County. The prosecuting attorneys were former Civil War generals Malcolm Patterson (then attorney general of Shelby County and later governor of Tennessee) and George Peters. The defendants were represented by another former general, Luke Wright (also prominent in state and national politics). The imprisonment and trial was a four-month-long "media circus" ending in the acquittal of the only two defendants for whom there was enough evidence to make a case. Even though almost 25 years would pass before another lynching, race would continue to be a major factor in Memphis' social, political, and economic life.

At the end of the nineteenth century, only 30 percent of black children in Memphis attended school.

8. THE GILDED AGE OF MEMPHIS

As the twentieth century turned, Memphis moved into the big leagues. Having annexed 12 square miles to the east and north in 1899, the city had quadrupled in size. The 1900 census revealed Memphis had eclipsed the 100,000 mark, surpassing Atlanta and Nashville. The 102,320 citizens were almost evenly split between black and white (48 percent to 52 percent).

The city owed much of its growth and prosperity to the fortuity of its location on the Mississippi River and in the center of the South. Construction of railroads in the 1880s and 1890s, including seven new lines into the city, and the Great Bridge (later named the Frisco Bridge) across the Mississippi, connected Memphis with the rest of the nation.

Sitting in the heart of the richest cotton region of the world and one of the most extensive hardwood forests in the United States, Memphis evolved as a hub of industry and distribution. Three-quarters of the nation's cotton was being grown within 200 miles of Memphis. By river and rail, cotton and lumber poured into the city, where it was classed, processed, turned into manufactured products, loaded onto riverboats and railroad cars, and shipped to buyers around the world. During rush season, between October and January, the streets on both sides and for several miles were piled high with cotton bales awaiting the cotton buyers, classers, weighers, clerks, and hands. The streets bustled with the ceaseless din of cotton-laden horse-drawn carts shuttling between Cotton Row and the paddlewheelers waiting on the cobblestone wharf. Hundreds of local lumber mills and manufacturing companies processed lumber into a wide variety of products: barrels, wagons, furniture, coffins, and hardwood floors. By the early 1920s, Memphis boasted more than 30 sawmills and E.L. Bruce had become the world's largest hardwood flooring manufacturer.

All this prosperity fueled a downtown building boom beginning in the 1890s and continuing through the 1920s. The city's first skyscraper—that is, with steel framing replacing masonry-bearing wall construction—was the 11-story Continental Bank building built in 1895. The bank failed shortly thereafter and the Porter family bought it as a memorial to their patriarch, D.T. Porter, who had been president of the Taxing District of Shelby County after the city lost its charter in 1879. Folks came to the big city and paid 10¢ to ride the region's first elevator to the rooftop garden of the D.T. Porter Building for the best view in town. It was soon topped by the 15-story Tennessee Trust Building at 81 Madison in 1905. By 1911, downtown Memphis bristled with a host of high rises, including the 18-story Central Bank and Trust, the 19-story Exchange Building, the 15-story Memphis Trust, and the 10-story Falls Building. Handsome brick and stone office buildings lined Second, Third, and Front Streets along with exuberant monuments like the Cossitt Library, the Gayoso House, and the Grand Opera House. Around the edges of the city arose the ostentatious mansions of the area's cotton rich. Memphis was a highly stratified society, with a few wealthy entrepreneurs and cotton merchants parading their wealth before thousands of clerks and laborers.

On the streets of the city carriages, wagons, buggies, electric streetcars, and a few horseless carriages bullied hapless pedestrians. Automobiles first appeared in Memphis in 1901 with only a few able to afford the $650 novelty. Still, by the end of the decade, there were about 1,000 automobiles in the city where the speed limit was 8 miles per hour. Most people relied on the extensive trolley system to get around. The Memphis Street Railway ran an extensive network of 150 cars per day over 109 miles of track.

Four-legged transportation was important too. Mules were highly valued for hauling commerce, and mule trading was part of the downtown business scene in

Merchants and brokers watch as workers load cotton bales and sacks of cottonseed onto the Sadie Lee at the Memphis levee.

75

Memphis until well after the First World War, with traders sometimes moving 1,000 mules a day. Barns were lined up along Third from Monroe to Union and along the north side of Union opposite the present site of the Peabody Hotel. The boom held through the World War, but collapsed when gasoline engines took precedence.

Horses were traded in Memphis as well. This was harness racing country, supporting two competing tracks. Montgomery Park, way out on Central and East Parkway, held races nearly every weekend. Memphis Driving Park, a private development of Memphis Street Railway heir C.K.G. Billings north of town, was a quarter-million-dollar showplace. Crowds of 10,000, many of them wealthy magnates arriving in private railway cars, came to watch and bet on the Memphis Gold Cup races, the final event on the Grand Circuit. Here the legendary horse Dan Patch set a mile record for pacer with silky at 1 minute, 56.25 seconds—a record that stood for 20 years. Such racing excitement came to an abrupt halt in 1906 though, when the Tennessee General Assembly made it unlawful to bet on "any trial or contest of speed or power of endurance of man or beast."[26] Locals continued to contest one another for the prestige of having the fastest buggies, but the thrill was gone and the driving parks soon closed.

In 1912, the city of Memphis acquired additional acreage without annexation, but at first no one wanted to claim it. Receding waters following a massive spring

Cotton drays share Main Street with trolleys and dozens of bowler-hatted pedestrians, c. 1900.

flood that inundated the north end of downtown revealed a large sandbar on Memphis' doorstep. It appeared to have formed from the confluence of two events: around 1876, some 20 miles above Memphis, the Mississippi River had shifted, altering the direction of the current flowing past the city. The second mitigating factor was the anchoring of the U.S. Navy gunboat *Amphitrite* near the mouth of the Wolf River. The Spanish-American warship was being transferred to the Missouri State Reserves to be used for student training in 1910 when it encountered low water at Memphis. For some 21 months, the ship remained parked, altering the silt patterns and causing a sandbar to form. Instead of disappearing when the ship left in 1912, each rise and fall of the river added silt and sand. Within a year, it extended from Court Street to Beale Street. Nonetheless, engineers assured worried Memphians, who feared it would jeopardize the future of the harbor and waterfront, that the river would soon scrub it away, yet the obstruction remained. During his campaign for the Senate in 1916, Kenneth McKellar pledged to get rid of it. The following year, the Mississippi River Commission authorized the removal of what was then being called Mud Island. (It is not technically an island, as it connects to Memphis on the northern end.) Yet by the mid-1920s, it had become a permanent fixture in the harbor. There it sat squat, ugly, periodically inundated, frequently struck by tugboats and steamers, more or less a huge island directly in front of downtown Memphis. It would be 70 years before someone figured out what to do with it.

Since its founding, Memphis had been a well-designed town, heedful of the need for public squares, wide boulevards, and scenic parks. In 1900, Memphis established a park commission with an ambitious mandate to redesign the city's original four squares (Court, Auction, Market, and Exchange), develop two new small urban parks (Forrest and Confederate), and design and develop two large new parks on the periphery of the city. By the end of 1906, the commission had purchased, designed, developed, and opened more than 1,750 acres of parkland.

For the major parks, the city purchased two large tracts: 445 acres along the river bluff south of the city and 342 acres of virgin forest in an area known as Lea's Woods east of town. These would become Overton Park, named for Overton Lea's ancestor John Overton, one of the original founders of the city, and Riverside Park. Although the larger one, Riverside Park (now called Martin Luther King, Jr.-Riverside Park) did not receive the attention Overton Park did. Intended to remain a nature park, it was remote and largely inaccessible in the early years. Folks wanting to enjoy Riverside Park needed to plan a day's journey, pack a picnic, and take an excursion riverboat to reach it.

Landscape architect George Kessler of Kansas City designed a showplace in Overton Park with winding drives, a large virgin forest, wide grassy meadows, and a lovely pavilion. A golf course was added in 1904. Upon the advice of landscape architect John C. Olmstead, stepson of Frederick Law Olmstead (designer of New York's Central Park), the commission voted to tie the two large parks together with an innovative system of parkways. East Parkway and South Parkway formed a 172-acre greenbelt encircling the city. Wealthy landowners along the route donated rights of way, no doubt driven by a combination of civic duty and awareness of the potential to increase their property values. And indeed Overton Park and the parkways soon became among the most desirable residential areas in Memphis.

At the north end of Overton Park, at the western terminus of Summer Avenue, the park commission built a "speedway." It was a measured mile, a drag-strip of sorts, for gentlemen to use in racing their buggies against one another. This was done to remove such activities from city streets in the interest of public safety, but was phased out when automobiles replaced buggies later in the decade. The street eventually became known as North Parkway, but it was not widened to match the other parkways until the mid-1950s.

Overton Park soon added bridle paths, a bandstand for concerts every evening at dusk, a golf course, and a zoo. Overton Park Zoo opened in 1908, having evolved without any city planning. It began in 1905, when A.B. Carruthers accepted a black bear cub in partial payment for a wholesale order of shoes from a Natchez, Mississippi retailer. He donated the cub as a mascot to a Memphis baseball team, who named him "Natch." It wasn't long before Natch grew beyond the cute stage and the team could no longer keep him. They muzzled the bear and chained him to a tree in Overton Park. Soon other people with surplus pets carried them to the park and lined the cages up next to the bear, creating a public menagerie. Mrs. Carruthers organized the Memphis Zoo Association in 1906 and began raising money to fund a permanent establishment. The first elephant, named Sara, came to Memphis in 1910.

In 1912, the Parks Commission acquired Montgomery Park racetrack as a permanent home for the Tri-State Fair, held in Memphis since 1856. To the Grand Carousel and Pippin roller coaster, obtained from the defunct East End Amusement Park (on Madison west of Overton), was added a host of exhibition buildings. The ten-day run of the fair (suspended on Sundays) featured agricultural products, livestock and horses, and a poultry show said to be the largest of its kind in the South. The women's department offered ribbons for food and handiwork and the midway featured the "living half-woman, half-alligator" and "the headless man," high-wire acts, trapeze artists, balloon races, and parachute jumps.

African Americans had attended and participated in the Tri-State Fair at least into the 1870s. Following the collapse of Reconstruction and the Supreme Court decision in *Plessy v. Ferguson* in 1896 that enshrined "separate but equal" and legalized segregation, blacks and whites in Memphis increasingly occupied two separate societies. Black city office holders, police officers, and school board members elected in the 1870s and 1880s gradually disappeared as the predominant Democratic Party pressed for white supremacy and used a variety of efforts to systematically disenfranchise black voters through force, intimidation, and legislative measures like registration laws and poll taxes. Half the population was forbidden to participate in the fair, attend the zoo, use the parks, visit the art museums, along with a host of other services and public facilities. In 1911, the Negro Tri-State Fair was organized, held at the fairgrounds a few days after the

Designed by the same landscape architect that fashioned Overton Park, Forrest Park was built on the site of the old City Hospital.

white fair closed. Some of the same acts and attractions stayed on. When the white fair changed its name to the Mid-South Fair in 1928, the black fair became simply the Tri-State Fair until it was discontinued in 1959. The Mid-South Fair was formally integrated in 1962.

The erosion of civil and political rights for African Americans went hand-in-hand with the city's infatuation with the Lost Cause. In 1901, Memphis hosted the Eleventh Annual National Reunion of the United Confederate Veterans. Citizens of Memphis raised an astonishing $80,000 to commemorate the surviving rebels with the construction of an 18,000 seat Confederate Hall on the site of Confederate Park near the river. One of the largest single donations came from the region's first black millionaire Robert Reed Church, whose $1,000 was hailed as a gesture of reconciliation by white leaders. The three-day reunion celebration culminated in a parade of 15,000 veterans through city streets draped in bunting and flags. The *Commercial Appeal* called it "the most imposing spectacle ever witnessed in the South."

Jim Crow laws separating blacks and whites on streetcars went into effect in the summer of 1905, shortly after the statue of Confederate General Nathan Bedford Forrest, slave trader and founder of the Ku Klux Klan, was dedicated in Forrest Park. The cornerstone for the park was laid in May 1901 during the Confederate reunion and a one-and-a-half times life-size bronze casting of Forrest astride his horse was commissioned at the cost of $32,359. His remains and those of his wife were disinterred from Elmwood Cemetery and reinterred in the park. Some 30,000 people representing seven states in the South attended the dedication ceremony on May 6, 1905. Three years later, the park commission turned the former city dump at the foot of Jefferson Street into Confederate Park, complete with Civil War cannons pointing toward the harbor. The statue of Jefferson Davis, however, was not added until 1964.

White neighborhoods and black neighborhoods developed separately and in different areas of town. While there were major black residential and business districts in North and South Memphis, Orange Mound, Binghamton, and Hollywood, the heart of black Memphis was Beale Street on the southern boundary of downtown. Widely known as "the Main Street of Negro America," this 15-block neighborhood was the center for business, politics, social and religious life, a vibrant collection of pool halls, saloons, banks, barber shops, dry goods and clothing stores, theaters, drug stores, gambling dens, jewelers, fraternal clubs, churches, entertainment agencies, beauty salons, hotels, pawn shops, blues halls, and juke joints. Above the street-level storefronts were offices for African-American business and professional men: dentists, doctors, lawyers, tailors, photographers, undertakers, teachers, and real estate and insurance brokers. Many whites, particularly recent immigrants, also lived and owned businesses in the neighborhood: Italians ran produce stands, grocery stores and theaters; Jews owned clothing stores and pawn shops; Greeks ran restaurants; Chinese owned laundries and restaurants. There were also Irish, German, and French merchants.

Without question, Beale Street's leading figure was Robert Church, Sr. He was self-educated and a shrewd businessman. He made his money primarily from investments in real estate, especially during the dim period following the Yellow Fever Epidemic of 1878. Buying up property from upper-middle-class whites moving further east, Church was largely responsible for the transformation of Beale Street into a vibrant center of the black community. In 1906, he established the Solvent Savings Bank and Trust Company, providing a sound financial base for black business development.

Since black citizens could not use the public park system, Church built one for them. Church's Park covered over six acres with formal walks and gardens with spectacular floral displays and wandering peacocks. Visitors enjoyed the picnic grounds, children's playground, and bandstand concerts on warm summer evenings. The centerpiece, the auditorium, could seat 2,200 people and featured one of the largest stages in the region. Traveling performers and vaudeville shows appearing in Church Park Auditorium included the Black Patti Troubadours, starring Madame Sissieretta Jones; the Smart Set with S.H. Dudley, advertised as "The Greatest Colored Show on Earth"; and the Fisk Jubilee Singers. In later years, the auditorium hosted world-acclaimed musicians such as Duke Ellington, Louis Armstrong, Count Basie, and Cab Calloway. It functioned as a community center for African-American political organizing as well as entertainment.

Robert Reed Church was the nation's first black millionaire; this photo taken at Atlantic City, New Jersey, c. 1900.

Church played host to President Theodore Roosevelt in 1902. Some 10,000 black and white citizens of Memphis heard the President speak in Church Park. Roosevelt had caused an uproar the previous year when he invited Booker T. Washington to dine with him in the White House. The *Commercial Appeal* published a scathing attack on the President, referring to Washington as an "Alabama coon" and concluding sadly that "there is no record of the fact that the room has been disinfected or even the chair, knife, fork, plate and napkin deodorized." Roosevelt's appointment of Robert Terrell, one of the first African Americans to graduate from Harvard, as the first black federal judge, increased the fracture in the Republican Party, particularly in the South, between the "black and tans" and the "lily whites," who wished to purge African Americans from the party. Roosevelt sought Church's advice and assistance in holding the black-and-tans together. Church's daughter, Mary, was married to Judge Robert Terrell. His son, Robert Church, Jr., gradually took over the family business, managing Church Park and Auditorium and working for his father at the Solvent Savings Bank and Trust. After his father died in 1912, Robert Church, Jr. shifted his focus toward politics, becoming an important leader in the Republican Party in Memphis and nationally.

By this time, the Beale Street business and entertainment district was in full swing. As lively at night as during the day, it thrummed with music and revelry. Six theaters—the Savoy, Pastime, Daisy, Grand, and Palace—in addition to

President Theodore Roosevelt, visiting Memphis in 1902, addresses a crowd in Church Park.

Church Auditorium featured black vaudeville and musical entertainers. While there was gambling in the back rooms of most establishments, high rollers flocked to the Hole in the Wall, the Midway, and the Panama. The street teemed with:

> sporting men, easy riders, sweet men and their women, fancy prostitutes, whores, snow pushers, conjure sellers, river men, cooks and housemaids, laborers and yard men, country people in to see the sights, musicians, gamblers, the famous and the unknown, Beale Street had them all.[27]

Everywhere, whether in clubs, saloons, juke joints, or on the street, there was music. A distinctive American genre called the blues evolved from African-American spirituals, ballads, ragtime rhythms, work songs, and field hollers and found a home on Beale Street:

> Where Good-Time Charleys strut under white lights and razor-men slink in the shadows. Beale Street—where the odors of sweet incense and "hot cat" are zephyrs of heaven—where cops' whistles, thumping pianos and mooning guitars ride the breezes blowing up from the old Mississippi. Beale Street—the happy street where the blues was born.[28]

Down at P. Wee's Saloon—named for four-and-a-half-foot tall Italian immigrant owner Virtilio Maffei, who was allegedly so strong that he bested professional boxers in arm wrestling—an accomplished cornet player and band leader named William Christopher Handy composed a campaign song for a young reform candidate for mayor in 1909. He called it "Mr. Crump":

> Mister Crump don't 'low no easy riders here.
> Mister Crump don't 'low it—ain't goin' have it here.
> We don't care what Mister Crump don't 'low, we gonna bar'l house
> anyhow.
> Mister Crump can go and catch hisself some air.

Handy published the song in 1912 as the "Memphis Blues," the first published blues composition. Desperate for money, Handy sold the rights to his song to a New York composer for $100. The composer added some lyrics, republished the song, and sold over 50,000 copies within a year. Although he didn't benefit financially from his hit, Handy gained national attention and earned Memphis the designation as the "home of the blues." He teamed up with lyricist Harry H. Pace to form the Pace and Handy Music Company on Beale where they composed such hits as "Yellow Dog Rag," "Joe Turner Blues," and "St. Louis Blues," which was an immediate hit and recorded by many artists for many years, including Bessie Smith and Louis Armstrong. In 1917, Handy published the "Beale Street Blues" with this apt description:

> The Seven Wonders of the World I have seen
> And many are the places I have been;
> Take my advice, folks, and see Beale Street first,
> You see pretty browns dressed in beautiful gowns,
> You will see tailor-mades and hand-me-downs;
> You will meet honest men and pickpockets skilled,
> You will find that business never closes until
> Somebody gets killed.

Handy eventually moved to New York, but he took the blues with him. And he frequently returned to Memphis to perform. Yet, like Memphis musicians in the past, and still today, the locals were less than impressed with Handy's virtuosity. After a whites-only performance at the Lyric Theater in 1921, the *Commercial Appeal* referred derisively to "Handy, the jazz king, and his aggregation of syncopated chop-suey noisemakers."

Some of the finest blues musicians were black women. Among the best were Alberta Hunter and "Memphis Minnie" McCoy. Hunter was born on Beale Street in 1895. Her mother was a chambermaid for Miss Myrtle and Miss Emma's Sportin' House on Gayoso Street. Her father, a pullman porter, died when she was four. At age 14, she ran away from Memphis to make her way in Chicago as a blues singer, becoming one of the most popular African-American entertainers in the 1920s. Her big hits included "Tain't Nobody's Biz-ness If I Do," "If You

Want To Keep Your Daddy Home", and "Bleeding Hearted Blues." Memphis Minnie was born Lizzie Douglas in Algiers, Louisiana, in 1897. Before she was ten her family moved to Walls, Mississippi, just south of Memphis, and as "Kid Douglas" she played banjo and guitar on Beale Street corners. Minnie was discovered in 1929 by a talent scout from Columbia Records while playing in a Beale Street barber shop. She was an inspired guitarist; male musicians gave her their highest praise: "she played like a man." Memphis Minnie recorded over 100 songs during her 30 year career, including "Bumble Bee," "Cherry Ball Blues," "Lay My Money Down," and "I'm Selling My Pork Chops (but I'm Giving My Gravy Away)."

Like much that went on after dark on Beale Street, blues music was considered disreputable among middle-class African Americans. According to Nat D. Williams, journalist, history teacher, and disk jockey, "it used to be more or less disgraceful to associate yourself with the blues. . . . the blues had to start up from the bottom and come up with a lot of dirt on it."[29]

W.C. Handy, trumpeter and composer, poses with his band in 1918. Handy signed this photograph for his esteemed friend Robert R. Church.

9. ON THE ROAD TO REFORM

Memphis was known far and wide as a sporting town, where one could find cheap liquor, high stakes gambling, fancy prostitutes, and a casual attitude toward violence. The city admitted having 504 saloons in 1903. In 1909, the *Commercial Appeal* complained, "street-walkers have been as thick as wasps in summer time," and police had given up on trying to control the use of cocaine, which was routinely sold in pharmacies in small flat containers called "lids" for 50¢. The newspaper also declared, "Killing is now the most thriving industry in this part of the country. They kill them next door to the city hall, and shoot them in the streets." Memphis had a murder rate of 47.1 homicides per 100,000 people when the national average was 7.2. Prudential Insurance Company labeled Memphis the "murder capital of America." City leaders blamed it on notions of Southern honor, transients, and rowdy blacks who were too drunk and drugged to control their passions. White against black violence was also common. In a famous incident in 1912, "Will Bill" Latura, a notorious saloon keeper, invaded a black bar and without provocation fatally shot six patrons. He became an overnight folk hero, and the jury took no time to acquit him. Latura was killed by police outside his saloon in 1916.

In the spring of 1917, Antoinette Rappel, a 16-year-old white girl was found raped, murdered, and decapitated. Within hours, the police arrested a black wood-cutter named Ell Persons who lived in the woods less than a mile from the murder scene. Persons allegedly confessed to the murder after 24 hours of police questioning, but just to be sure they had the right man, the police used a new technique developed by a French scientist who claimed photography could reconstruct the last image seen by the victim. Rappel's eyes were photographed and although the image was blurry, Memphis authorities concluded that the girl's pupils revealed Persons' forehead and hair. The front page of the *Commercial Appeal* announced his guilt with lurid headlines and suggestions for proceeding: "MOB CAPTURES SLAYER OF THE RAPPEL GIRL; Ell Persons to be Lynched Near Scene of Murder; MAY RESORT TO BURNING." Readers were informed that the lynching was to take place between 9:00 and 9:30 that Tuesday morning near the Wolf River Bridge.

After the event, the newspaper described the festivities: "A crowd of some 5,000 men, women and children cheered gloatingly as the match was applied and a

Lieutenant George W. Lee, political activist and promoter of Beale Street, posed for this photo c. 1920.

moment later the flames and smoke rose high in the air and snuffed out the life of the black fiend [*sic*]." When the body had been "burned sufficient [*sic*] to satisfy the lust of the executioners, one man in the crowd cut out the negro's [*sic*] heart, two others cut off his ears, while another hacked off his head." Spectators snatched pieces of Persons' clothing and the rope that bound him. His head and one of his feet were thrown from a passing car into the midst of a group of African Americans standing near Beale Street.

The lynching of Ell Persons was the last in a series of publicly sponsored acts of violence against blacks that began with the 1866 riot. This horrific crime mobilized the black community to form the Memphis chapter of the National Association for the Advancement of Colored People (NAACP) and to organize politically in the Lincoln League. Led by Robert Church, Jr. and his associate Lieutenant George W. Lee, the League organized clubs in each black ward and held weekly meetings in Church's Auditorium. The League saw their grievances as "wholly political," and their agenda clear: to encourage blacks to claim and use their elective franchise and their collective political clout to secure social justice for their race. The League taught the fundamentals of voting, registered black voters, raised money to pay poll taxes, and put up black candidates for congressional and state offices. Church then expanded the group nationally into the Lincoln League of America. At the first national convention in 1920, 400 delegates from every section of the country met in Chicago to fight the evils of disenfranchisement, Jim Crow, and lynching.

Women, too, were mobilizing, although few were addressing civil rights. Women's activism began in late nineteenth-century Memphis with efforts to rescue "fallen women" and eliminate the scourge of demon rum. Elizabeth Avery Meriwether and her sister-in-law, Lide Smith Meriwether, flouting all rules of ladylike decorum, were at the forefront of these movements. Elizabeth was the first woman in Tennessee to publicly champion voting privileges for women, holding meetings on the subject in Memphis theaters in the 1860s. In 1872, after reading that Susan B. Anthony, attempting to vote in Rochester, New York, was arrested, tried, and fined, Meriwether announced she intended to vote in Memphis at the next election, expecting the same fate. Yet when Elizabeth walked into the Fifth Ward polling place, she was handed a ballot, she filled it out, then dropped it in the ballot box. She was never certain why she was not opposed, but she was clearly disappointed. Lide took prostitutes into her home and expressed public outrage over the sexual double standard while Elizabeth lobbied for equal pay for female teachers. Under Lide's guiding hand, the Women's Christian Temperance Union (WCTU) persuaded 6,000 citizens to pledge abstinence, including many of the city's most prominent men. By 1886, black women had established their own chapter of the WCTU with Mrs. C.H. Phillips, wife of the pastor of Collins Chapel Church, as president. One early success of the temperance forces was in 1877 with Tennessee's Four Mile Law, making it unlawful to dispense intoxicating beverages within 4 miles of a school. Buoyed by their success, the women in the WCTU, in conjunction with the Anti-Saloon League, sent out thousands of letters, collected thousands of signatures on

Ladies of the Nineteenth Century Club meet in splendor to choose their philanthropic projects.

petitions, and lobbied throughout the state in support of a prohibition bill that passed the Tennessee General Assembly in January of 1909.

Temperance activism spawned interest in a number of other issues related to home and family. Throughout the first two decades of the twentieth century, a host of white women's organizations, including the King's Daughters, the Nineteenth Century Club, and the Women's Christian Association, focused on a broad array of social problems. They raised money for hospitals and libraries, schools and homes for widows and orphans, like the Protestant Widow's and Orphan's Asylum (later called Porter-Leath Children's Center). They invaded the jails, asylums, poorhouses, and hospitals to direct attention to the women housed there.

Black women had their own social and reform associations like the Daughters of Zion, the Coterie Migratory Assembly, the Phillis Wheatley Club, the Ruth Circle, and others to build and sustain churches, care for orphaned children, the sick, and elderly, and to promote education. Black women formed settlement homes for recent migrants to the city and founded the Old Folks and Orphans Home on the old Hernando Road. Black and white women worked in concert on a number of issues, including temperance, suffrage, and prison reform. Led notably by Julia Hooks, sometimes called "the Angel of Beale Street," organized black and white women secured a women's matron for female prisoners. They also got involved in politics, calling attention to widespread gambling and prostitution, campaigning to clean up cocaine abuse, lobbying for improving employment and labor conditions, and demanding the ouster of corrupt officeholders.

Reform was in the air, and riding the wave into office under the reform banner in 1909 was Edward Hull Crump. His was a true Horatio Alger story: a poor, Mississippi farm boy comes to Memphis with 25¢ in his pocket in the decade following the yellow fever epidemic. He quickly establishes a lucrative harness business, marries into the prominent and prosperous McLean family, and rides the groundswell of public indignation about high taxes, inadequate police and fire protection, and government corruption into the mayor's office in 1909 by a margin of 75 votes. He establishes a profitable and efficient political machine that enables him, though he was more often out of office than in, to control the city's destiny for the next 45 years.

As a candidate, he pledged to reorganize the fire and police departments, improve efficiency in municipal government, to remove the "easy riders," gamblers, pimps, and prostitutes, and to curb crime. He accomplished his first two objectives; what's more, he also took control of the Shelby County government. By 1911, the Shelby County Quarterly Court had an unwieldy and inefficient 50 members. Crump superimposed control with a three-member executive committee overriding the court on most matters. The easy riders, though, hardly paused and the murder rate increased. By 1916, it had risen to 89 murders per 100,000 people, again the highest in the nation. Crump never promised to abide by prohibition and he didn't. He became mayor the same year prohibition passed in Tennessee, but Memphis was a liquor distribution center. Local brewers and

These three women, Mrs. Robert Reed Church, Jr, Mary Church Terrell, and Annette E. Church, pictured here in 1911, were actively involved in reform efforts.

distillers, as well as large liquor companies, had a great deal of local political clout. Crump argued that he was simply following his constituents' wishes and he could prove it. After he publicly announced he would not enforce prohibition, he was reelected in 1911 and 1915. The law finally caught up with him just after his last reelection when then governor Ben Hooper pushed through a law providing for the removal of public officials from office who refused to enforce the state's laws. The ouster petition revealed Crump had set up a very profitable system to circumvent the law. Every Monday morning, saloon keepers, madames, and gambling house operators showed up at City Court to pay the maximum penalty of $50. The city treasury collected significant funding and the payoffs were made openly and legally as fines. Caught red-handed, Crump resigned his office just hours before court action would have removed him. The next day all saloons and gambling halls were closed, but a few months later the *Commercial Appeal* reported that whiskey could still be had "in a hundred places" around town.

Out of office, Crump kept his highly efficient, well-financed machine rolling, placing his hand-picked candidates in all municipal and many state offices, on the strength of the huge quantity of votes he could deliver. City employees campaigned house-to-house for Crump candidates and blacks, many dead or fictitious, swelled the rolls.

Memphis was the only Southern city where African Americans were not disenfranchised. In other Southern cities, Democratic primaries had become white primaries, but in Memphis, blacks held as much as a quarter of all the city ballots. While not nearly enough to control elections, as long as black voters could

Robert Church, Jr. and Oscar DePriest stand in front of Church's office on Beale Street. DePriest, the first black congressman elected since Reconstruction, represented Chicago from 1929 to 1935.

influence the outcome, they had to be courted and given some patronage. While many African Americans continued to vote Republican, the party of Lincoln, there was no "black voting block" that could be delivered by either side. Black voters expressed a good deal of initiative, voting for what they considered their own best interests.

On the Republican side of the ledger, Robert Church, Jr., because of his close ties to the national party, was able to deliver considerable federal patronage to black Republicans as long as his party was in control in Washington. Church and his closest political subordinates, George W. Lee and Dr. J.B. Martin, invested considerable energies into educating and registering African Americans to vote. Church served as a delegate to eight consecutive Republican National conventions, from 1912 to 1940. Republicans held the presidency from 1896–1912 and 1920–1932. Because of Church's power, for example, 123 of the 159 mail carriers during the 1920s were African American.

"Boss" Crump was a firm believer in blacks' right to vote as long as they voted for him. His machine used payoffs from liquor and vice interests to pay the $2 poll tax, which had been instituted specifically to keep blacks from voting. The machine held the receipts until election day before distributing them to reliable voters. This proved very effective in delivering huge numbers of votes to whomever Crump chose. For example, in 1936, Gordon Browning won election as governor with the help of 60,218 votes from Shelby County—only 861 went to his opponent. Crump's machine also won a large share of the legitimate black vote with a host of services: supplying free milk to babies of indigent parents, curbing police abuse of African Americans, bestowing assorted city jobs, investing in public housing and black schools, developing 53 acres northeast of the city into Douglass Park, and opening Overton Park and Zoo to blacks one day a week (Thursdays). Crump was, in short, a classic big city "boss," using his power to harass and hound his enemies, while establishing a progressive city government with low taxes, good schools, top fire and police services, and efficient government. The overwhelming majority of Memphians, black and white, were happy to let Mr. Crump manage their city.

While allowing, indeed helping, blacks to vote, Crump also supported woman suffrage. Lide Meriwether established the state's first woman suffrage league in Memphis in 1889 and carried its message across Tennessee. With the turn of the century and women's reform efforts came new confidence, a sense of mission, and the absolute conviction that in order to be able to fix the ills of society they would need the franchise. Memphis, for many decades, had been a bastion of pro-suffrage sentiment in Tennessee, turning out big, reliably responsive audiences for touring national suffrage leaders. Both daily newspapers favored votes for women, as did Memphis' state representatives. This comfortable consensus was likely due, at least in part, to the discipline of the Crump machine that regularly achieved unanimity in support of various issues coming before the legislature by imposing the so-called "unit vote rule" on lawmakers whose elections the machine had sponsored.

Memphis hosted a series of suffrage celebrations every spring, marked by an explosion of yellow (the suffrage color) sashes, bunting, banners, and streamers that bedecked the trees, light posts, and grandstand in Court Square. The

Edward Hull Crump at the beginning of his long political career as the "Boss" of Memphis.

91

celebrations reached a crescendo in 1916 when Carrie Chapman Catt, president of the National American Woman Suffrage Association, came to town for two days of events designed to launch, said the *Commercial Appeal*, a "sweeping campaign . . . to gain enfranchisement for women in Tennessee as early as possible."

At Main and Madison, in front of a huge electric sign reading "VOTES FOR WOMEN," a large group of women defied convention and spoke to what were then called "promiscuous crowds"—that is, including both males and females. Some 350 attended a luncheon at the Hotel Chisca that, according to the *News-Scimitar*, was "one of the most brilliant functions ever given during a conference in the city." In the evening, the *Commercial Appeal* breathlessly reported: "Several hundred men and women who filled the Lyric Theater to its capacity were converted to the cause of suffrage last night. Some of the audience were ardent suffragists before the meeting. Others were not, but now they are." Most of the people in town lined up expectantly on Main Street for the "monster parade" Wednesday afternoon. They were not disappointed, said the newspaper, for it was "a parade, which for its effulgent splendor would have awakened the envy of the late Phineas T. Barnum."

Though there was no mention of black women in the Memphis suffrage pageantry, many African-American women recognized the vote as critical not only to their quest for equality, but also for racial uplift and social justice. National suffrage leaders Susan B. Anthony and Carrie Chapman Catt addressed black women in Memphis at a series of meetings sponsored by the Coterie Migratory Assembly in 1895. Working mostly through established clubs, black women attended political meetings, signed suffrage petitions, and encouraged black men to pay poll taxes and vote. Despite cooperation on a host of issues affecting their gender, black and white women divided over issues that reflected their racial identities, making solidarity across racial lines impossible to sustain.

Interestingly, the two most prominent black women involved in the suffrage battle nationally were from Memphis, though their public activities happened far from the city. These two women, Ida B. Wells and Mary Church Terrell, were the only women among the original founders of the NAACP in 1909. Ida B. Wells fled Memphis in 1892 to mobilize an international movement against lynching. In 1913, Wells founded Chicago's Alpha Suffrage Club, the first organization for black and white suffragists. Mary Church left Memphis to attend Oberlin College in Ohio, then married Roosevelt appointee Robert Terrell. As the first president of the National Association of Colored Women's Clubs, Church asked her "sisters of the dominant race [to] stand up not only for the oppressed sex but also for the oppressed race!"[30]

After the 19th Amendment, granting women the right to vote, passed Congress in 1919, 36 states were required to ratify it before it became law. In the summer of 1920, Tennessee was the last battleground. The Shelby County delegation, including representative T.K. Riddick and floor leader Joseph Hanover, led the protracted and difficult fight for the Tennessee General Assembly's approval. The *Nashville Tennessean* called it "the bitterest, bare-fisted, name-calling, back-biting session in the state's history." The Senate was safe with votes to spare, but everyone knew the contest in the House would be extremely close—and it was. On a steamy August day, the measure passed by a vote of 50 to 49. The deciding vote was cast by the youngest member of the assembly, Harry T. Burn, whose mother had urged him to vote for suffrage. Tennessee became "the perfect 36," the 36th and final state needed to ratify the 19th Amendment, and in doing so instantly enfranchised 27 million American women.

Harry Burn, the youngest representative in the Tennessee Assembly in 1920, cast the deciding vote for woman suffrage upon the advice of his mother.

10. GROWING PAINS

Out on the periphery of the city limits—so far out that the Memphis Street Railway had to extend their lines to take workmen to the site—the West Tennessee State Normal School, a state teacher's college, opened in two red brick buildings on 80 acres of cotton fields in 1912. Beginning with 12 faculty and 330 students, the school became Memphis State College in 1941 with 950 students. Tuition was about $19 a quarter. After earning university status in 1957 and integrating in 1959, Memphis State enrollment surged past 20,000 in the 1970s where it remained through the 1990s. In 1994, the name was changed to The University of Memphis. Southwestern College, a private Presbyterian institution, moved to Memphis from Clarksville in 1925, erecting a lovely array of Gothic structures of Arkansas limestone on a 100-acre campus northeast of town. It was renamed Rhodes College in honor of Peyton Nalle Rhodes, president of the school from 1949 to 1965, after his death in 1984.

African-American institutions of learning included most notably LeMoyne Normal Institute, which originated as a Freedman's School in 1871 and had 600 students in 1915 in a variety of academic departments. The University of West Tennessee moved from Jackson, Tennessee, to Memphis in 1907. Its black students studied medicine, dentistry, pharmacy, law, and nurses' training. The Baptist Bible and Normal Institute, which came to be called the Howe Institute after its largest donor, was organized in Memphis in 1888. In addition to religious training, Howe's curriculum offered academic and vocational training in sewing and nursing for girls, and construction skills for boys. According to the *Commercial Appeal*, "This school makes a specialty, for one thing, of furnishing trained houseboys for the people of Memphis—sending into this service as many as 100 a year."

In 1916, an entrepreneur named Clarence Saunders opened Piggly Wiggly at 79 Jefferson Street and changed the way Americans buy their groceries. Before Saunders, shoppers entered tiny stores and asked the clerk at the counter to retrieve whatever they needed from the items in bulk storage in the back. Clerks dipped pickles from barrels, measured out flour, and sliced wedges from wheels of cheese as the customer requested. At the Piggly Wiggly, customers entered a turnstile near a bin of wicker baskets and followed a circuitous route through the

Entrepreneur Clarence Saunders never lived in his pink limestone mansion. After building Piggly Wiggly grocery stores into a nationwide chain, he lost ownership of both the stores and the house. Acquired by the city, the structure now houses the Pink Palace Museum.

store, selecting what they wanted from rows of products neatly arranged on shelves and toted them to the "paying station" at the end of the line. Among the innovations Saunders introduced in his patented "self-serve" stores were consumer-size packaging, price tags attached to every item, and the inclusion of a meat market and a produce market within his store with refrigerated cases to keep these items fresher longer. He also mastered the art of modern advertising. For several weeks before his first store opened, he bought billboards around town stating only that "Piggly Wiggly is coming." No one knows why he chose the name. One story claims he was inspired by the sight of some little pigs struggling to go under a fence. Asked why he chose such an unusual name, Saunders replied, "So people will ask that very question."

Piggly Wiggly was a big hit with customers, offering more efficiency and lower prices than his competitors. Saunders franchised his concept, and by 1923 the chain included 1,268 stores selling $100 million in groceries, the third largest retail grocery business in the nation. Out east, on 160 acres along Central Avenue, Saunders built a mansion out of pink Georgian marble at a cost of nearly $1 million. He called it Cla-Le-Clare after his three children: Clay, Lee, and Amy Clare. Before the mansion was completed, following a series of complex stock transactions, Saunders lost control of his grocery empire and his pink palace. His estate was sold to local businessmen who developed the area into Chickasaw Gardens and the city turned his home into the Memphis

In 1919, Memphis celebrated the centennial of its founding and America's victory in World War I with a parade of gaily decorated automobiles and floats. In honor of the day, Memphis dubbed itself the "Wonder City of the South."

Museum of Natural History and Industrial Arts, but folks always called it the Pink Palace.

Piggly Wiggly was only the first of three chains Saunders developed. He immediately went right back into the grocery business with "Clarence Saunders, Sole Owner of My Name Stores" or Sole Owner Stores. Although these were successful, the Depression forced him to close the chain after nine years. Then, in 1937, he designed and constructed a prototype for an automated store based on vending machines, which he called the "Keedoozle" (for "Key Does It All"). The customer slipped a key into a coin slot next to a window display. The key activated circuits that released the merchandise to tumble onto conveyer belts in the warehouse. The groceries were delivered to the cashier's window, then on to the loading dock where the customer picked them up. The idea was to dispense groceries quickly and efficiently while tracking inventory, but mechanical failures forced them to close in 1941. Until the time of his death in 1953, Saunders was developing plans for another fully automated store system called the "Foodelectric."

True to the spirit of "the Volunteer State," nearly 9,000 Memphians, or more than a third of Shelby County's eligible population, joined the army after America entered the Great War. Everyone called it the Great War until there was another world war 20 years later. The youngest American soldier to see combat was a Memphian named Albert Cohen. He enlisted at age 13 and was killed in action on the Western Front two years later.

The city launched a coordinated home-front mobilization under the state's Council of Defense. They registered women and non-eligible men for war work and urged citizens to buy bonds to support the boys in France. The war turned out to be a great stimulant for local businesses. Mule traders sold 10,000 animals to the French government in 1914 alone. Cotton trading during the war increased significantly, with local brokers selling more than 1 million bales during the war. The military services established training and procurement facilities in the area. The Army Signal Corps began teaching men to fly at a landing strip on the infield of the Memphis Driving Park, then built Park Field at Millington to train pilots and ground crews.

For Americans, the war was a short one. Having raged in Europe since 1914, it was 1917 before the United States sent troops to France. Still, Memphis lost 230 young men in the Great War. Their names are posted on the 1917–1919 Honor Roll at Overton Park. The Daughters of the American Revolution funded the

Phoebe and Vernon Omlie, barnstormers in the 1920s, settled in Memphis to establish the first airport in the mid-South. Phoebe went on to fame as an air racer and was the first woman to earn a transport pilot's license and an aircraft mechanic's license.

Doughboy statue there in 1926 to honor "the memory of Memphis and Shelby County men who gave their lives to their country in the Great War."

After the war, many military fliers tried to make a living in aviation. They took up "barnstorming," flying around the country putting on airshows and offering rides, but it was a hard and dangerous existence. Phoebe and Vernon Omlie, popular barnstormers from the upper Midwest, drifted south in the fall of 1921, looking for warmer weather and more opportunity. They offered rides at the old airstrip at the Driving Park and began drawing together a clique of air-minded Memphians, many of them World War I veteran fliers like Vernon, to talk about the future of aviation in Memphis.

At the veterans' reunion on Armistice Day in 1925, they founded the Memphis Aero Club. Pooling their money, the group leased 70 acres of cow pasture at Woodstock and named this first airport in Memphis after Guion Armstrong, an air casualty of the war. The Omlies stopped barnstorming and set up Mid-South Airways at Armstrong Field, offering flying lessons and, beginning in 1928, round trips to Chicago three days a week for $60. Charles Lindbergh landed at Armstrong in October 1927 on his nationwide tour with the *Spirit of St Louis*. The newspaper reported 100,000 people lining the streets of Memphis as the aviation hero made his way to a big fete in his honor at the Peabody Hotel. There he joined the Aero Club in urging the city of Memphis to make a commitment to usher in the air age in West Tennessee. By the end of the decade, the goal was reached. Memphis Municipal Airport was dedicated July 14, 1929, with a sod field runway, three small hangers, and Vernon Omlie in charge.

The positive Memphis economy also spurred a post-war building boom downtown. Seven new buildings went up in 1924 alone: the Union Planters

Vernon Omlie became manager of the new municipal airport, which featured a sod runway and three small hangars, when it opened on the eve of the Great Depression.

Building at Union and Front, Lowenstein's Department Store, the Cotton Exchange, the Columbian Mutual Tower and the Claridge, Adler, and Peabody Hotels. At 22 stories, the Columbian Mutual Tower was the tallest in Memphis, at least for five years, until the spectacular 29-story Sterick Building was completed in 1929.

Retail stores crowded downtown side-by-side with banks and office buildings. Along Main Street alone sat a host of large department stores: Lowenstein's, Goldsmith's, Bry's, John Gerber, Oak Hall, Julius Goodman and Son, Woolworth's, and Kress. All of them had segregated restrooms, drinking fountains, and dressing rooms in a practice that lasted into the 1960s.

On September 1, 1925, the new Peabody Hotel flung open its doors on Union. The original Peabody, built in 1869 at Main and Monroe, had burned in 1923 and been torn down to make way for Lowenstein's Department Store. The 12-story Peabody, with 625 rooms, was much larger than its predecessor and much more elaborate, with a lavish banquet and ball for some 1,200 guests. It quickly became the premier hotel in Memphis. Historian David L. Cohn famously remarked:

> the Mississippi Delta begins in the lobby of the Peabody Hotel and ends
> on Catfish Row in Vicksburg. . . . If you stand near its fountain in the
> middle of the lobby, where ducks waddle and turtles drowse, ultimately
> you will see everybody who is anybody in the Delta.[31]

The celebrated ducks were added sometime in the 1930s when general manager Frank Schutt and his hunting buddy, auto dealer Chip Barwick, brought back some live decoy ducks from their hunting trip to Arkansas and plopped them in the extravagant fountain in the lobby. They remain to this day, ceremoniously marched with trumpet fanfares across a red carpet twice a day to the elevator for their trip to their rooftop roost, "the Duck Palace," in the evening and back the next morning.

Down at the north end of Front Street, John Philip Sousa was the opening act for the new Memphis Auditorium and Market House—a combination athletic arena, concert hall, convention center, and retail produce market. Apparently, city fathers didn't believe entertainment alone would sustain the huge investment, so they rented market stalls that, in the first ten years of operation, earned more money than the rental of the hall. The moving force behind the auditorium was Robert R. Ellis, for whom the facility was renamed in 1930. Ellis Auditorium hosted circuses, opera and symphony concerts, trade shows, movies, conventions, and big bands like Paul Whiteman and Guy Lombardo. Blacks had a separate side entrance and sat in a separate balcony. In segregated Memphis, the Harlem Globetrotters set record sales of more than 6,000 white tickets in 1953. The record lasted, however, only one day. The next night, 7,000 paid to see Gorgeous George wrestle Farmer Jones. The card also included Mildred Burke against Ella Waldek. Elvis Presley also played Ellis Auditorium in 1956. The facility was razed in the 1990s to make way for the new Cannon Performing Arts Center, which opened in January 2003.

The Travertine marble fountain in the elegant lobby of the grand Peabody Hotel is home to a famous troop of ducks that are escorted with great fanfare to the lobby in the morning and return to their Duck Palace on the roof each evening.

By the mid-1920s, in the hustle-bustle of downtown streets, trolleys were giving way to automobiles. Memphis had more than 200,000 citizens and many of them were behind the wheel. The streets became so treacherous that at one point Memphis had the third largest automobile death rate in the country and police began to arrest anyone going faster than 25 miles per hour. In 1947, the trolleys were retired and replaced with buses. By June, the last of the streetcars made their last run on the National Avenue line.

Automobiles also meant roads and development eastward. Suburbanization began in the 1920s as retail moved northeast of the city with the completion of the massive Sears and Roebuck Catalog Order Plant and Retail Store in 1927 on North Watkins. Though the heart of retailing in Memphis would remain downtown until the 1950s, the shift had already begun. Grocery stores, too, began moving out of downtown, opening branches in the neighborhoods. First Piggly Wiggly, then Kroger, who moved into the Memphis market by purchasing 57 of Saunders' former stores. Another major grocer, Seessel's, remained downtown until opening its first suburban store on Union Avenue in 1941.

By 1920, Memphis had one of the largest medical complexes in America. The University of Tennessee Colleges of Medicine, Dentistry and Pharmacy, founded in Nashville, moved to Memphis and merged with the Memphis Hospital Medical College and the College of Physicians and Surgeons in 1911 at about the same time that Baptist Memorial Hospital was being built. St. Joseph's Hospital, which opened in 1889, expanded to 300 beds by 1920. They were joined by Methodist Hospital in 1918. The complex also included the Regional Medical Center, "The Med," which began as Memphis General Hospital, initially chartered in 1829 to care for transients and paupers. The John Gaston Hospital, endowed by its namesake restaurateur, replaced the antiquated Memphis General in 1936. Private hospitals were all single race: St. Joseph's, Methodist, and Baptist treated only white patients. Collin's Chapel Hospital and Gailor Clinic treated African Americans. Public John Gaston Hospital had separate wards attended by separate staff for black patients.

The wonder of radio came to Memphis in 1923 when WMC "Down in Dixie" went on the air—at least some of the time. The station fired up at 9:45 a.m. with the opening markets, the weather, and the river stages and positions of Federal Barge Lines tow-boats. Then there was silence until the noon market reports and a bit of music, perhaps from the "Skyline Serenaders" from the Peabody Café. Then more silence until the closing markets about 3:00 p.m., followed by silence again. At 8:00 p.m. there was a bedtime story for the children, but the big entertainment was an evening concert broadcast for an hour at 8:30. At times it was the Britling Novelty Orchestra from the cafeteria at Madison and Second, conducted by Frank Bracciante, who everybody called "Chin Chin." On other occasions it was the Hotel Gayoso orchestra with vaudeville singer Fred Hughes. After more silence, WMC was back on the air at 11:00 p.m. with dance music. It was all locally produced with local talent, and there were no commercials. The station was supported as a public service by the *Commercial Appeal*.

From an early start as nickelodeons on Front Street, movie theaters came into their own during the 1920s. Charles Dinstuhl opened his Theatorium on North Main, right next door to his confectionary in 1905, with a double feature: *The Great Train Robbery* and *If Benjamin Franklin Would Come Back to Life*. The movies even moved into the neighborhoods in an early form of the drive-in, except that these were walk-ins. Taking advantage of the mild Memphis weather, these theaters—actually little more than benches surrounded by wooden fences—were called Airdomes and at least a half-dozen were functioning during the war years. Downtown, people flocked to the movie palaces such as The Lyric, the Majestic, Warner, and Loew's State.

The grandest theater of them all was the Orpheum. Built on the site of the Grand Opera House at Beale and Main, the theater was part of the Orpheum Circuit for vaudeville shows, hence the name. It hosted some of the biggest names in live theater including Dick Powell, Virginia Dare, Mae West, and Houdini, who escaped from a locked box thrown into the Mississippi River. In

1923, a fire broke out during a show featuring a striptease artist named Blossom Seeley and burned the theater to the ground. It rose from the ashes five years later, with $1.6 million invested in its enormous crystal chandeliers, brocade draperies, and gilded moldings to become one of the grandest motion picture palaces of the era. Downtown theaters accommodated both races, but blacks had separate side entrances and could sit only in a separate balcony. Just up Beale Street, a number of theaters like the Palace, the Daisy, the New Daisy, and the Handy showed movies for blacks during the week and hosted live entertainment on the weekends.

Baseball was an important spectator sport in both the black and white communities, with each developing their own teams and franchises. In 1919, Beale Street barber A.P. Martin established the Memphis Red Sox baseball team. Martin sold the team to undertaker R.S. Lewis in 1922, who in turn sold it to Dr. W.S. Martin, a successful surgeon, in 1932. The Martins were one of the most prominent black baseball families in America. W.S.'s brother owned and operated the Chicago American Giants and another brother, dentist B.B. Martin, served as the Red Sox general manager. The team was a tremendous source of pride in the black community. The Red Sox barnstormed around the country playing white teams in exhibition games, and played to overflowing crowds at Martin Stadium (near what is now Crump and Danny Thomas) as part of the Negro American League. Mostly blacks attended the games, but there was a small section reserved for white spectators. The team thrived for some 40 years, from 1919 to 1959, although attendance began to fall off dramatically after Jackie Robinson broke the major league's color line in 1947. The Memphis Chicks, the white AA Southern Association minor league team, played at Russwood Park. Built on the site of the Red Elm Bottoms field, home of the old Memphis Turtles, the stadium opened in 1921. The Chicks played there for 40 years until the grandstand burned in a spectacular fire on Easter Sunday, April 17, 1960. A new stadium, named for Chick's catcher Tim McCarver, a hometown boy that made good in the big leagues, housed the Memphis Chicks until 1997 when, following a rash of ownership changes, the team moved to Jackson, Tennessee. The following year Triple A baseball and the Memphis Redbirds established a home in Memphis.

In 1925, black Memphian Tom Lee became a local legend when he rescued 32 white passengers from a capsized riverboat. Lee, a field hand and levee worker, was in his skiff, the *Zev*, headed upriver from Helena, Arkansas, to Memphis. About 20 miles south of the city, he passed the steamer *M.E. Norman*, which, Lee noticed, was listing to one side. Suddenly the low side slipped beneath the water and the strong current rolled the boat over. Most of the 72 passengers were thrown free to struggle in the cold swift water. Lee hurriedly pulled survivors out of the water until he had all his small boat could hold. Then he rushed them to the bank of Cow Island and went back for more. By dark he had saved 32 men, women, and children from drowning; 17 got themselves to safety and 23 drowned in the disaster. Lee was a genuine hero, acting quickly and without regard for his

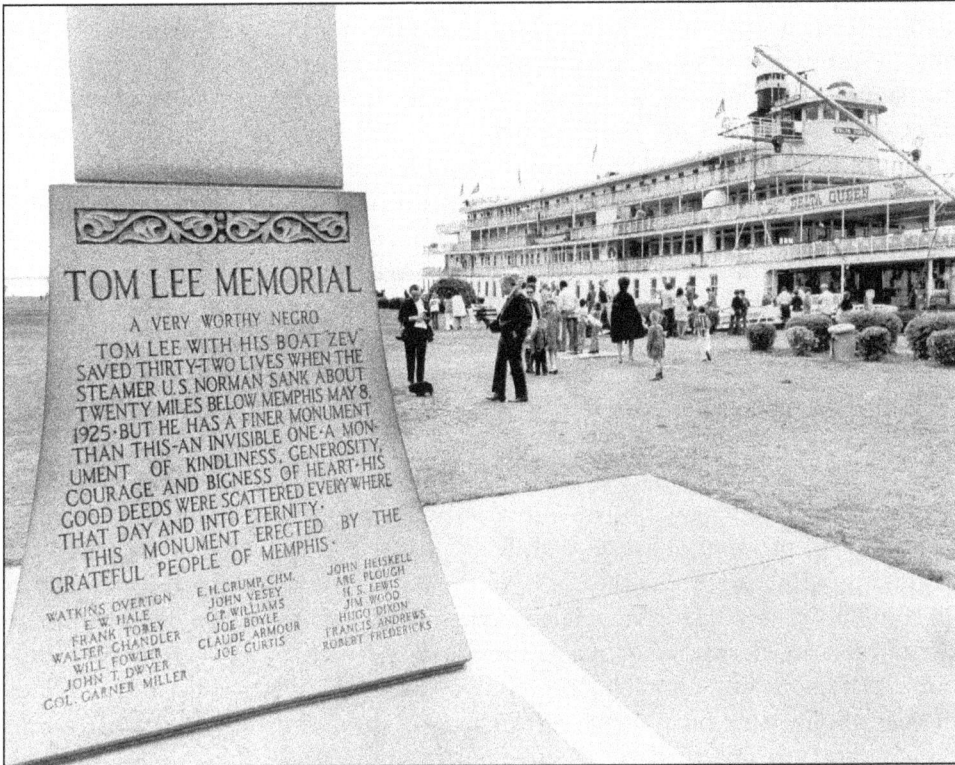

The city's monument to hero Tom Lee thanks him for his "kindliness, generosity, courage and bigness of heart" in saving 32 men, women, and children from drowning in 1925.

own safety; Lee could not swim. The grateful city presented Lee with a watch, a steady job with the sanitation department, and a trip to Washington to meet President Coolidge. Newspaper and civic groups raised $3,000 to buy and furnish a small home for him at 923 N. Mansfield, where he lived with his wife for the remaining 27 years of his life. After his death, Mayor Crump made arrangements for a monument to Lee, "A Very Worthy Negro," to be erected in the park named for him along the Mississippi (formerly Astor Park) for his "kindliness, generosity, courage and bigness of heart" from "the grateful people of Memphis."

Society changed rapidly after the end of the World War I. America became infected with a devil-may-care, live-for-today attitude that city fathers and religious leaders were determined to staunch in Memphis. A sign of society's deterioration appeared at the Tri-State Fairgrounds, where the city had opened a new municipal (white-only) swimming pool. Shocked that men and women were allowed to swim at the same time, with women wearing tight-fitting, immodest bathing suits, the Shelby County Baptist Association pronounced it "a veritable hellhole."[32] In 1924, the Girl Scouts sponsored a night of folk and square dancing, or attempted to. When the Protestant Pastors Association protested that the Bible forbids dancing, the scouts regrouped and renamed their activities "rhythmic games." H.L. Mencken designated Memphis "the buckle on the Bible belt" as a host of spiritual revivals and prayer meetings were called to bring citizens back to the straight and narrow. In April 1924, the city erected a huge temporary tabernacle at Jefferson and Front Streets for the arrival of evangelist Billy Sunday. He spoke to over 85,000 Memphians during his week-long visit, and what a show it was. The first night, 25,000 people crowded inside while hundreds more were turned away, including African Americans who would hear Sunday in a segregated arena. Sunday denounced modernism, pacifism, Bolshevism, evolution, jazz, and the sins of the city. He planned to "go after all the rottenness, meanness, filth, and vice of this town." At one point, according to the *Commercial Appeal*, Sunday "tore off his coat, smashed a chair to emphasize his contempt for Russia, leaped upon a table, pounded the ceiling with his fist and dared the Devil to seven weeks combat in an open field."

In 1928, the city appointed Lloyd T. Binford, president of the Columbian Mutual Life Insurance Company, to a one-year term to head a three-member Board of Censors to ensure that Memphis citizens were not exposed to degrading influences at the theater or in the movies. Binford was reappointed to 28 consecutive one-year terms. Given absolute power "to prevent the exhibition of immoral, lewd, and lascivious pictures, acts, performances . . . inimical to the public safety, health, morals and welfare," Binford gave thumbs down on all movies or plays that featured excessive violence, plunging necklines, unpatriotic themes, and most particularly, positive portrayals of black life or scenes showing blacks and whites together.[33] Memphians never got to see, for example, *Duel in the Sun, Miss Sadie Thompson, Forever Amber, The Wild Ones, Rebel Without a Cause*—at least not in the city. Films banned in Memphis were often shown in West Memphis, so folks would cross the river to see them. In 1945, Binford blocked *Annie Get Your Gun* from Ellis Auditorium simply because there were black performers in the cast. Other movies were minutes shorter when they were shown to Memphis audiences because Binford insisted that scenes with black performers—like Lena Horne, Pearl Bailey, and Cab Callaway—be snipped out. He prevented the screening in 1936 of the prizefight between Joe Louis and Max Schmelling. National magazines spotlighted Binford; *Time* observed that "Binford has long prided himself on being able to spot a suggestive line even before it was suggested," and *Colliers* called him "an extreme case of capricious and mischievous interference with the freedom of adults." Nonetheless, Lloyd Binford protected Memphis audiences until the mid-1950s when he retired.

Another sign of the reactionary times was the revival of the Ku Klux Klan. Unlike the early Klan founded by former Confederate General Nathan Bedford Forrest, this one, organized at Stone Mountain Georgia in 1915, was a reaction to a changing social order in primarily urban areas. This new Klan attacked European immigrants, Catholics, and Jews, as well as African Americans. Memphis, by 1923, had 10,000 members organized into local Klan Number 3, and the Klan entered formal politics with a candidate for mayor and a slate of candidates for other local offices. Throughout the campaign season, the Klan staged marches and demonstrations, and on election day, Klansmen stood in every voting place, handing out literature and harassing voters. Largely because of the opposition and power of Crump, and the war against the Klan carried out by *Commercial Appeal* editor C.P.J. Mooney, all but one of their candidates lost. While Crump was as committed to white supremacy as anyone, his machine depended upon the votes of blacks, Jews, and Irish and Italian Catholics. Mooney and political cartoonist J.P. Alley were awarded the Pulitzer Prize in 1923 for their expose of the Klan's depredations.

In this shot of Main Street and Madison, taken in 1912, automobiles, buggies and pedestrians jockey for space with a string of electric streetcars. On the left is Pantaze Drug Store.

11. Depression and a New Deal

The Booming Twenties soon gave way to a decade of despair. Though the Stock Market Crash is considered to mark the beginning of the Great Depression, in Memphis hard times started earlier, particularly for farmers and the businesses that depended upon agriculture. The flush times ended with World War I when demand dropped and export markets dried up, driving the poorest farmers off the land. Tractors and mechanical cotton pickers displaced field hands by the thousands and spurred an exodus of black and white sharecroppers to the city, swelling the population by 40,000. There they found unemployment and hunger. Families doubled up, crowding into dilapidated structures. Fully half of the city's inhabitants (77 percent of blacks and 35 percent of whites) lived in substandard housing. Over 70 percent of them used communal outdoor toilets or pit privies. Squatters built shelters in open fields and out on Mud Island.

Mud Island had been steadily growing, despite periodic efforts to eradicate it. By the 1930s, it was a mile and a quarter long and a mile at its widest point; it flooded when the river passed 27 on the Memphis gauge. City fathers zoned the island in the 1930s to keep out industry and officially renamed it "City Island," though no one called it that. Because the island was so frequently inundated, squatters mounted their scrap lumber and tar paper shelters on huge logs or empty oil drums or the rotting hulls of abandoned houseboats. Even the barns and chicken houses were built on floats. By the end of the decade, the squatters, a mix of black and white, numbered at least 200 and perhaps as many as 500 and had established what they considered to be permanent residences. It was not until 1964 that the island was ordered vacated in anticipation of development.

A number of local entities had the bad luck to build or expand just as the economy took a dive. The Sterick Building, a 29-story, Gothic-style, gleaming white wedding cake of a building costing nearly $3 million, opened with great fanfare on the eve of the Depression and was one of the first major buildings to go bankrupt in 1932. The Memphis Municipal Airport faltered as air travel became an expensive luxury few could afford. In 1930, only 15 passengers were arriving and departing daily. Air mail and freight barely kept the airport open. The failure of the black-owned Fraternal and Solvent Savings Bank and Trust in 1927 sent shock waves through the African-American community. The result of a merger just two months before of Solvent Savings, established in 1906, and Fraternal Savings Bank, established in 1910, the institutions were both heavily invested in real estate loans that turned sour along with the national economy. The 28,000 depositors received only 9¢ on the dollar in the liquidation proceedings.

Private charities were overwhelmed with too many needy and too little with which to help. Salvation Army records show they fed 1,700 in 1929, 8,200 in 1930, 10,250 by March of 1931. The city had no money and no way to collect taxes. The Mayor's Commission on Unemployment and Relief formed in 1930. The commission gave apples to 80 men to sell on the street and employed a few to chop firewood and distribute it to the needy. Blacks participated in the program under the direction of "Colored Division" director George W. Lee, who held benefit shows at Beale Street theaters, but funding quickly dried up and the Relief Commission folded in 1932. The Community Welfare League that followed was also largely unfunded and dependent upon charitable contributions. The suicide rate provided a grim barometer of the situation. Historian Roger Biles wrote "so many people were jumping off Harahan into the Mississippi that the newspapers printed the names and telephone numbers of clergymen and urged the dispirited to seek counseling. Soon a Memphis preacher jumped off."[34] The Memphis school system

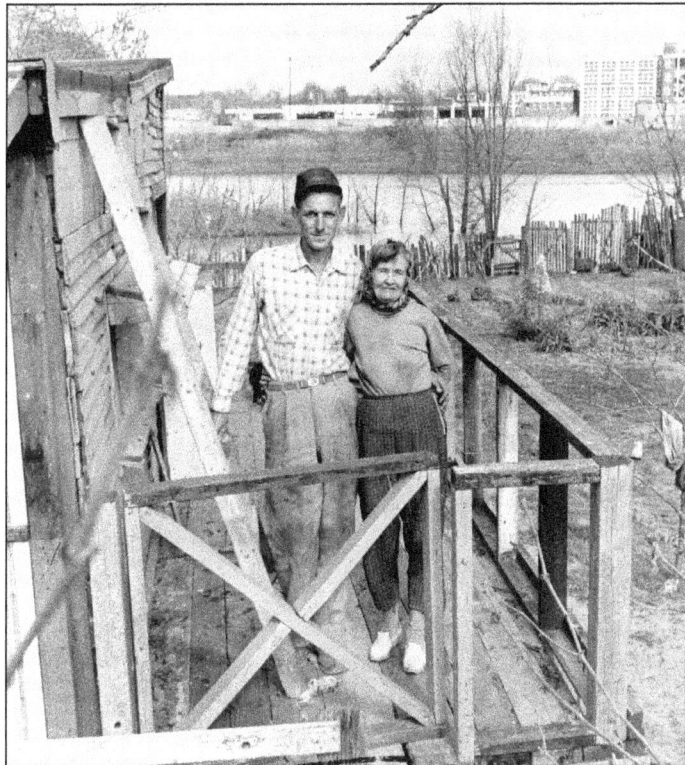

"The Queen of Mud Island" Effie Wingate and her husband William Moshier pose in front of their ramshackle home built of scrap lumber, tin, and tarpaper on Mud Island. They were part of a large community of squatters (variously estimated from 200 to 500) who resided on the island until 1964 when they were forcibly removed.

ran out of money in 1932, cutting teachers' already low salaries by 16.75 percent and paying them in scrip, substitute money accepted only by some businesses.

The cotton market bottomed out in 1933. Selling at 5¢ per pound, the distribution market was clogged with a three-year supply of unsold cotton. Cotton factors and merchants, desperate to find ways to revive their fortunes, came up with a celebration called the Cotton Carnival. Patterned after the Memphis Mardi Gras, celebrated from 1872 to 1892, and omitting the religion, the First Cotton Carnival was held in March 1931. During "Cotton Week" all stores and theaters displayed cotton and cotton products in their lobbies and store windows and sponsored newspaper ads and radio programs to tout Memphis' most important product. On the final day, as music played and fireworks streaked in the sky, the royal barge glided along the river carrying the King, Queen, and Royal Court, composed of young women mostly in their first year of college. The Queen was another young woman "at least a couple years older," and the King a prominent business leader. Cotton Carnival royalty, marching bands, flower-bedecked automobiles filled with dignitaries, and 86 floats constructed by students from Tech High gathered at Ellis Auditorium, then swept down Main Street through the business district, crossed over to Second and returned to Ellis. The theme was "The Old South," featuring Southern belles and gallant Southern

Cotton Carnival celebrated Memphis' relationship to cotton with pretty girls and elaborate floats with Old South themes. Horses, automobiles, and in this case, black men, towed the floats through the streets.

gentlemen. Black women, dressed as mammies, perched on bales of cotton aboard the floats or greeted passers-by on street corners. Teams of black men, along with horses and mules, pulled the floats through the streets as thousands of eager spectators packed shoulder-to-shoulder to cheer them on. While it is not clear that the carnival had much impact on the cotton market, it did become a major social event in the city. Secret societies composed of Memphis' elite planned ever more elaborate celebrations each year.

African Americans, denied participation in the festivities except as beasts of burden, responded five years later with a celebration of their own role in Memphis' cotton prosperity. Begun in 1936 by Beale Street dentist Dr. R.Q. Venson, the Beale Street Cotton Maker's Fiesta soon came to be known as the Cotton Makers' Jubilee. The week-long celebration featured the Jubilect (a talent show and election of royalty) a beauty contest to choose the Bronze Maid of Cotton and Miss Sepia Venus of the Mid-South, a Red Sox baseball game, and three parades: a children's parade, coronation parade, and the Grand Jubilee Parade. The parades began at the foot of Beale Street at Riverside Drive and ended in Handy Park. The Cotton Makers' Jubilee focused on African themes with floats depicting ancient Egypt and ancient West African civilizations; the royalty dressed as Pharaohs and consorts, accompanied by girls in grass skirts and painted warriors. Beale Street's chief export, music, also figured prominently in the Jubilee. W.C. Handy served as its first grand marshal and the Booker T. Washington High School Drum and Bugle Corps in their green and gold uniforms always dazzled the crowd.

From its inception, the Jubilee had support from the white community, who welcomed the black community's separate celebration of cotton. Cotton Carnival organizers served on the advisory board of the Cotton Makers' Jubilee and white royalty appeared on the platform with black royalty, but the reverse was not done. In the 1960s, the NAACP and student activists picketed the Jubilee for its inappropriate celebration of cotton and, by implication, slavery. Yet it continued to thrive.

In 1981, after the Cotton Carnival had replaced their secret societies with krewes (organizations patterned after New Orleans' Mardi Gras to manage and stage the Carnival festivities), they invited the Cotton Makers' Jubilee to become a krewe and a full partner in the Carnival. For the first time, African-American royalty were presented to the Crown and Sceptre Ball. Although the barges and parades are gone, the societies continue the tradition of choosing royalty for what is now called Carnival Memphis and hold a series of social functions capped by the Grand Carnival Ball every June. The Jubilee retains its appeal in the black community and in 1999, the name was officially changed to the Memphis Kemet Jubilee. Kemet, an Egyptian word meaning black, was determined to be "a more befitting, descriptive, and historically significant name." The Kemet Jubilee currently extends for ten days in May.

Franklin Delano Roosevelt accepted the Democratic nomination for President in 1932 by promising "a new deal for the American people." This New Deal put people to work who had no source of employment. With Democrats in power in

The City Beautiful Commission made housekeeping a part of city pride. To dramatize their "clean-up, fix-up" campaign in 1941, they held a parade featuring pretty girls with brooms and garbage cans, and 50 painters climbed on scaffolding at Gailor Hall on Poplar to paint the whole building pearl-gray in five minutes.

Washington, Memphis' leadership was poised to collect a disproportionate share of New Deal goodies. E.H. Crump was elected to Congress in 1931 with 90 percent of the vote and stayed two terms. As a freshman, Crump had minimal clout in Washington, but in combination with Tennessee's senior senator, Kenneth McKellar, he exerted tremendous influence in obtaining projects and programs to revitalize Memphis' industry and infrastructure. McKellar had been in Washington since 1911 and in the Senate since 1916. His considerable seniority had earned him the chair of one of the most important Senate committees, Appropriations. In short, he controlled the money. His symbiotic relationship with Crump, which extended to the beginning of both of their political careers, ensured that Crump would deliver the local support while McKellar was extremely skilled in attaining federal money to promote economic development in Tennessee.

The Public Works Administration (PWA), created in 1933, was the first national peacetime effort to create jobs. While African Americans were eligible for these and many of the alphabet agency New Deal programs, their administration was controlled by the local machine that did nothing to upset existing racial arrangements. More than $8 million of PWA money poured into Memphis, building the John Gaston Hospital, a new grain elevator, juvenile court, dormitories at the University of Tennessee Medical School, and several public schools. PWA projects improved streets, parks, bridges, sewers, and drainage ditches. In conjunction with the Army Corp of Engineers, the PWA built "the most expensive highway in the world" in downtown Memphis, Riverside Drive.

For years the area along the river had been a garbage dump and the bluffs were prone to erosion and occasional cave-ins. In 1926, a chunk of the bluffs—100 feet wide and 700 feet long—between Butler and Nettleton Street, broke off and fell 50 feet into the river, taking houses, the railroad tracks, and an entire coal company along with it. It took five years to clean up the trash and stabilize the bluff. Then, in an amazing allocation of cash in the midst of the Depression, the federal government, local landowners, and the Illinois Central and Frisco Railroad invested $1 million to build Riverside Drive. The mayor's nine-year-old daughter cut the ribbon on a spring day in 1935 and a parade of cars moved along the road, escorted by boats on the river and airplanes overhead. The Men's Garden Club of Memphis planted 100 ginkgo trees and 50 flowering crabapple trees along the route. The City Beautiful Commission later added hundreds of magnolias, crepe myrtles, redbuds, dogwoods, and roses.

The City Beautiful Commission had been appointed by Mr. Crump in 1930 to make housekeeping a central part of city planning. Appropriately, he put ten prominent housewives in charge and gave them $1,500 to get started. Chairwomen in each of the city's 52 wards, in cooperation with women's clubs, both black and white, spearheaded efforts to clean, paint, trim, and landscape the city. They crowned a "Crepe Myrtle Queen" every year and awarded trophies and

Automobiles parade down the newly completed Riverside Drive, escorted by trains on the bluff. The most expensive highway in the world when it opened in 1935, Riverside Drive provided a link between downtown and the Harahan bridge over the Mississippi River.

certificates in competitions for backyard beautification, window-box gardening, business landscaping, and mini-parks in vacant lots. Largely through their efforts, Memphis was voted the cleanest city in Tennessee seven times (1940–1946) and the "Nation's Cleanest City" in 1948, 1949, 1950, and 1951. Memphis was also named the nation's quietest city throughout much of the 1950s, thanks to the passage of a law during the Crump era banning the use of automobile horns except in cases of emergency, a tradition that continues to this day.

PWA funds also changed the landscape of Memphis. Although they were not yet using those terms, these were the opening projects for urban renewal. Two large public housing projects were built on cleared bayou areas that once held substandard housing adjacent to downtown. Built at a total cost of $6.2 million, Lauderdale Courts had 449 units for whites and Dixie Homes had 663 units for blacks. Both projects opened in 1938. Three additional housing projects were funded at the end of the decade: Lamar Terrace with 478 units for whites opened in 1940; William H. Foote Homes with 900 units, and LeMoyne Gardens with 500, both for black residents only, opened in 1940 and 1941. The projects were controversial at the time because in many instances they displaced at least partially middle-class black neighborhoods.

In the spring of 1935, just as Riverside Drive was opening, the federal government, responding to public clamor for more dramatic action, created the Works Progress Administration (WPA). Similar to the PWA, the WPA concentrated on infrastructure improvements: building bridges, streets, highways, and public buildings. Over 8,000 WPA workers in Memphis performed extensive road and street work, painted buildings, resurfaced sidewalks, landscaped parks. Larger projects included the new Crump Stadium, a bandshell at Overton Park,

Large housing projects financed by New Deal monies, like Dixie Homes and Lauderdale Courts (pictured here), were hailed as a solution to slums in Memphis. The Presley family of Tupelo, Mississippi, moved there with their young son, Elvis, in 1949.

improvements to the Zoo, and important additions to the municipal airport, including three diagonal asphalt runways and a new terminal building.

Another of the New Deal alphabet agencies, the Civilian Conservation Corps (CCC), established a camp in Collierville in southeast Shelby County. The CCC employed America's youth with conservation and environmental projects by planting trees, building shelters, and restoring parks and historic battlefields. Although the CCC, like all New Deal programs, had a non-discriminatory policy, this was ignored in the South by administrators who insisted on maintaining racial separation. Two CCC camps were established, one for whites and a smaller one for blacks. In 1939, a CCC crew was cleaning up T.O. Fuller State Park when they discovered an archeological treasure, a site "literally ankle-deep in crumbling bones, bricks and ancient pottery." The WPA's team of archeologists uncovered a large Mississippian village, apparently occupied for about 3,000 years, with ceremonial and burial mounds dating from approximately 1000 to 1400. The Chucalissa Village was arranged around a central plaza, dominated by a large ceremonial mound for the dwelling of the chief, and surrounded by smaller mounds for lesser leaders. In 1962, the village, reconstructed to portray Native American life *c*. 1400, was transferred to the University of Memphis to operate for research and educational purposes.

One of the more important New Deal projects for Memphis was the passage of the Flood Control Act of 1937, signed six months after a disastrous flood in February. For most of its history, floods had been a constant source of anxiety and hardship for Memphis and efforts to hold back the river were a continuous struggle. A massive flood in 1912 breached earthen levees, putting block after block of neighborhoods under water, contaminating city water, and threatening a typhoid epidemic. Over 30,000 people received typhoid shots. The floodwaters measured 45.3 feet on the Memphis gauge, 5 feet higher than the previous record. Another flood in 1913 collapsed the North Memphis levee and submerged 20 blocks along Bayou Gayoso. Mayor Crump turned the Tri-State Fairgrounds into "Camp Crump" to provide food, shelter, and first aid to black refugees for more than six weeks before they could return to their homes. New levees were constructed and these held even when the greatest flood in history struck the Mississippi Valley in 1927. At 45.8 feet in Memphis, the flood inundated some 2.3 million agricultural acres, forced 700,000 people from their homes, took 214 lives and caused a $1 billion damage. Relatively secure atop the bluffs, downtown Memphis was practically untouched by the waters, but many neighborhoods north of the city were underwater. Moreover, with the city's economy tied to cotton and hardwood production in the valley, Memphis was seriously affected by the disaster. The fairgrounds again became a refugee camp, this time for white people, for folks from as far away as Kentucky and Illinois. Secretary of Commerce Herbert Hoover toured the disaster area and the Coolidge administration sent $5 million in disaster aid and a commitment to a comprehensive plan of levees, floodways, and channel improvements from Cape Girardeau, Missouri, to New Orleans.

Ten years later, the river rose again, cresting at 48.7 feet, almost 3 feet higher than had ever been seen before. On February 1, 1937, the river was 3 miles wide in Memphis. The waters drove 270,000 from their homes, seriously injured 900 people, and 250 died of drowning or other flood-related causes as the Mississippi, the Cumberland, the Tennessee Rivers, and their tributaries overflowed. The business district and downtown were safe atop the bluffs, but the north end along the Wolf River and the southern end along Nonconnah Creek were submerged. The flooding would have been much worse if it were not for the quick mobilization of thousands of WPA and CCC workers, National Guardsmen, highway patrolmen, and volunteers working around the clock to build and stabilize makeshift levees. When Crump got word that the Nonconnah levee was in danger, he donned hipboots and led hundreds of WPA workers and 500 penal farm prisoners to throw up a flood wall. He also sent the police to round up blacks on Beale Street to "volunteer" to help in the emergency, some of them still dressed in their Saturday night finery.

The city set up a refugee camp at the fairgrounds where up to 60,000 people—the majority who were sharecroppers and river-town residents—were fed, housed, and given medical care. Twelve schools were turned into makeshift hospitals. Cases of influenza and pneumonia were widespread and approximately 8,000 were hospitalized in Memphis. At the height of the emergency, Crump telegraphed Senator McKellar in Washington to plea for "levees, pumping stations, and seawalls" to be built around Memphis so that such a disaster would not occur again. Congress responded with legislation authorizing a $9 million flood-control project for Memphis. Thousands of men were put to work constructing concrete and steel-reinforced levees to protect the city from waters up to 55 feet.

Also thanks to McKellar, Memphis was a prime beneficiary of one of the largest New Deal projects, the Tennessee Valley Authority's (TVA) system of dams and inexpensive hydroelectric power. In order to tap into the power, the city needed a distribution system funded by bonds approved by voters. On November 6, 1934, the measure was supported by a margin of 18–1, and in celebration the city renamed Maiden Lane, a narrow alley downtown, to "November Sixth Street." Power from the TVA became available in 1939, the same year the city acquired Memphis Power and Light, adding in the city-owned water and gas utility to form Memphis Light, Gas and Water (MLGW). Crump had been attacking the private power company since taking office, wanting lower rates and public ownership. After Memphis Power and Light lost their suit challenging the constitutionality of the TVA as a publicly owned utility, they gave up and sold out to the city.

Crump was at the peak of his power and determined to further weaken his nemesis Robert Church, Jr. Church's control over Republican patronage mattered little during the New Deal. Moreover, many African Americans, in Memphis and elsewhere, were shifting their allegiance away from the party of Lincoln to that of Roosevelt. In 1940, when Church actively campaigned for Wendell Wilkie, whose election could restore Church's power, Crump moved to

Floods were a constant threat to Memphis until the completion of the massive New Deal flood control project. These families were stranded on the levee during the 1912 flood.

destroy Church by seizing his real estate holdings allegedly for failure to pay property taxes. Church fled to Washington as the city changed the name of Church Park to Beale Avenue Park and burned Church's home to test new firefighting equipment. Similarly, Crump moved against Church's political associates, druggist J.B. Martin and café owner Elmer Atkinson, stationing police outside their establishments to search all customers who entered. The police commissioner wrote letters to black leaders, accusing them of "presumptuous ingratitude" and warning them, "This is white man's country, and always will be, and any Negro who doesn't agree had better move on."[35]

Lieutenant George W. Lee remained the Republican voice in Memphis but many Memphis black voters shifted their allegiance to the Beale Street Democratic Club headed by Dr. J.E. Walker, founder of the Universal Life Insurance Company and one of the city's wealthiest entrepreneurs. Walker, having been rebuffed by Bob Church for a position at the Republican National Convention in 1932, organized a Negro Democratic Club and began working with the Crump organization to share New Deal largess with the black community. Lieutenant Lee continued to be active in Republican national politics.

In 1952, he was chosen to give a seconding speech for the nomination of Robert Taft against Dwight Eisenhower, the first time a black politician had addressed a National Republican convention since Reconstruction. In 1960, as he battled John Kennedy for the presidency, Richard Nixon visited Beale Street under the sponsorship of Lieutenant Lee.

At Beale and Hernando, after razing the old Market House, the city built a small park in 1931 called the Beale Street Square. Lieutenant George W. Lee decided it would be only fitting to name the park for the father of the blues, W.C. Handy. After lengthy negotiations, Crump agreed. On March 29, 1931, Lee and Handy rode together at the head of the parade followed by 2 miles of marching bands and fraternal clubs, all stepping to the "Beale Street Blues," to dedicate Handy Park. Though no longer a resident of Memphis, Handy returned to the city every year for the high school Blues Bowl featuring the football teams of the two black high schools, Booker T. Washington and Manassas. After Handy's death in 1958, the city commissioned a statue of the famous musician and placed it in the park May 1, 1960. The park was refurbished in 2000 with construction of a new open-air theater, dressing rooms, public restrooms, and an information center, and rededicated in October 2000.

Other local celebrities making headlines in the 1930s included Machine Gun Kelly (George Kelly Barnes) and Richard Halliburton. Machine Gun Kelly became the FBI's "Public Enemy Number One" in 1933. Like his contemporaries Baby Face Nelson and Pretty Boy Floyd, Kelly was a Prohibition-era thug most noted for successfully avoiding capture by local authorities. Then he made his big mistake. In 1933, not long after the Lindbergh baby was kidnapped and murdered, a law was passed making kidnapping a federal offense. In the same year, Kelly decided to abduct an Oklahoma oilman and hold him for ransom. Though the FBI poured into Memphis in hot pursuit, it was local policemen who nabbed Kelly, who was hiding out in a midtown home. After waiting all night for a raid that didn't come, Kelly let his guard down in the morning. When police showed up at his front door in broad daylight and found it unlocked, they surprised Kelly in his hallway in his underwear without a gun. Kelly surrendered quietly.

Richard Halliburton made his claim to fame without breaking the law. He grew up in Memphis, graduated from Princeton in 1921, then became a world traveler and adventurer, as well as renowned lecturer and writer, thrilling readers in a series of best-selling books about his exploits. His 1925 bestseller was called *Royal Road to Romance*. Then came *New Worlds to Conquer, Glorious Adventure, The Flying Carpet,* and *Seven League Boots.* By the time he was 35, Halliburton had climbed the Matterhorn and Japan's Mount Fuji in winter, swam the entire 50-mile length of the Panama Canal, climbed Popocatepetl in Mexico, retraced the route of Ulysses as described in Homer's *Odyssey,* crossed the Alps on an elephant, probed Yucatan's Mayan Wall of Death, and circumnavigated the world in a small bi-plane. An excursion in March 1939, at the age of 38, proved to be his last. While sailing his 75-foot wooden junk, *Sea Dragon,* from Hong Kong to San Francisco to prove that Asian explorers could have ventured across the Pacific to America, he encountered a typhoon. He sent a radio message on March 23 and was never heard from again. His father, a businessman who had been instrumental in moving Southwestern College to Memphis, gave the school $400,000 to build the Halliburton Memorial Tower on the campus of what is now Rhodes College. At the base of the tower is a plaque memorializing "A Wonderful Life of Action, Romance and Courage" and likening Halliburton to the Greek legend of Icarus: "He Flew Too Near the Sun."

The legacy of the great bluesman is preserved in Handy Park at Third and Beale. The park was established in 1938. The bronze statue was placed in the park on May 1, 1960, two years after Handy's death.

12. THE SECOND WORLD WAR AND THE FABULOUS FIFTIES

Citizens of Memphis, like most Americans, responded with patriotism and resolve when the Japanese attack on Pearl Harbor in December 1941, thrust America into war. So many volunteers showed up at the recruiting station in the Post Office that it was staffed 24 hours a day to handle the 160,000 Shelby County residents who registered for service. One-quarter (40,000) were inducted for active duty; 662 of those men lost their lives in World War II.

Just like the soldiers in uniform, people on the homefront had a job to do. They volunteered for civil defense duty, bought war bonds, donated blood, collected old newspapers and scrap metal, and planted victory gardens. Families who had sent a son or daughter into the service proudly displayed a blue star in their window. Those who received the dreaded War Department telegram that began "I regret to inform you . . ." substituted a gold star. Everyone did their part. Memphians recycled tin cans, household fats, old pots and pans, and children turned in pencil stubs so the graphite could be recycled for war production. A host of materials needed for the war effort—gasoline, tires, and food staples like sugar and coffee—were rationed. Wartime shortages led to creative ways of doing without conveniences. Once silk was no longer available and nylon was needed for parachutes, ladies were required to give up their stockings. Some women resorted to beige leg make-up and drawing seam lines down the backs of their legs with eyebrow pencils. Everyone was encouraged to be thrifty and reuse everything.

In its zeal to promote recycling of rubber, tin cans, and metal, Memphis was probably the only city to use authentic Civil War artillery to fight World War II. Six cannon, four squat mortars, and a stack of Civil War cannon balls from Confederate Park went into the melting pot of the scrap metal drive. Also donated to the cause were two captured German field pieces that flanked the Doughboy Statue in Overton Park and an ancient Spanish cannon from Court Square, cast in Seville in 1795, captured by American forces in Cuba in 1898.

Some 30,000 farm workers, black and white, increasingly displaced by agricultural mechanization, poured into Memphis to work in the military facilities and war industries. The absence of men, especially acute late in the war, opened up new opportunities for women around the country. They worked in factories as riveters, welders, drill press operators, and a host of other previously all-male jobs "for the duration." Most of the employees at the Chickasaw Ordnance Works Plant, operated by DuPont on Shake Rag Road north of town, were women. Built at the cost of nearly $25 million, the massive complex had more than 100 buildings and kept 8,000 people working around the clock to make TNT and smokeless gunpowder. It opened with a contract for the gunpowder from the French and British governments in 1940; the contract was eventually taken over by the United States. The Memphis Street Railway also hired women drivers for buses and operators for street cars during the war.

Memphis industries converted to war: Firestone stopped producing automobile tires and began manufacturing rubber life rafts and tires for the army; Ford shut down its auto assembly line and began producing airplane engines; International Harvester produced vehicles for the army; Fisher Aircraft Division of General Motors built wings and fuselages for bombers; Continental Can Company manufactured shell cases; Plough, Incorporated, produced pharmaceutical products for the military; and Kimberly Clark produced cellu-cotton products. When rubber became scarce after the Japanese conquest of Malaya and the Dutch East Indies, an

E.H. Crump poses with two soldiers among the dozens of wounded soldiers and sailors he took as guests on his annual boat ride in 1943.

entire new industry for synthetic rubber was born. The Quaker Oats Company in Memphis manufactured furfural alcohol needed to make synthetic rubber.

Crump and McKellar attracted a good deal of national defense spending for facilities in the Memphis area. The Second Army Headquarters relocated from Chicago to Memphis; The Fourth Ferrying Group Command Base was headquartered at the Memphis airport. In 1942, the $17 million Army Quartermaster Defense Depot opened on Airways. One of the largest military facilities in the world, the depot was a huge complex of 103 warehouses, covering 642 acres and employing 5,000 people. In the same year, the air force built a depot on Jackson and the navy transformed old Park Field at Millington into the largest inland naval base in the country, including the Naval Air Station, Naval Air Technical Training Center, and the Naval Hospital. Also in 1942, construction began on Kennedy General Hospital, a sprawling 4,600-bed complex for war casualties on 160 acres at Park and Shotwell Avenue. They soon changed the unfortunate name to Getwell. By the end of the war, over 44,000 wounded and ill soldiers were treated at Kennedy. After also serving as a Veterans Administration facility, the hospital property was acquired by the University of Memphis in 1967 after the VA relocated their hospital downtown.

While the war raged in Europe, Memphians closely followed the exploits of the *Memphis Belle*. Named for Margaret Polk, the Memphis girlfriend of the

This wartime parade was held to promote war bond sales in the city.

pilot, Captain Robert H. Morgan, the *Belle* was a B-17 Flying Fortress, one of the largest American planes in the war with a 104-foot wingspread. The *Belle* became the first B-17 to complete 25 missions over Europe and return to the United States under its own power with its original crew. The ten-member crew shot down eight enemy fighters and earned a total of 51 decorations. Although it had been damaged repeatedly in raids, requiring seven new engines, two new wings, and a tail section, the plane's record was remarkable at a time when chances for success were slim. The *Belle* was part of the 324th squadron of the 91st bomber wing, a group that required 95 percent replacements during the nine months the *Belle* completed its 25 missions. The romance between Morgan and Polk became one of the best known love stories of the war, featured in *Life* magazine and made into a Hollywood movie, but it didn't last. The *Belle* disappeared, too. Scrapped after the war, a reporter discovered it in Altus, Oklahoma, where he recognized its distinctive nose art. Memphis mayor Wyeth Chandler bought the plane for $350 and a promise to refurbish and display it. Amazingly, it was still flyable. The *Belle* came home to a pedestal in front of the National Guard Armory on Central Avenue in 1950. Since 1987, it has been parked in an open-air pavilion on Mud Island, where the elements and the birds have taken a toll. A consortium of devotees plan to make it the centerpiece of a $10 million World War II museum east of the city.

As soon as wartime shortages eased, construction of the new Memphis-Arkansas Bridge began in 1945. This four-lane highway bridge would replace the old Harahan and end the often terrifying experience of traversing the Mississippi River along a narrow pair of one-way wooden spans hung on the outside of the old bridge. Another major project on the river was the Tennessee Chute Project for development of Presidents Island. Like Mud Island, the 900-acre strip of land was often a hazard to navigation, periodically swamped in high water, and a haven for squatters and bootleggers. The Chute had once been the main channel of the river; building a causeway-dam across it created a sheltered deep-water harbor on McKellar Lake and turned Presidents Island into a major industrial freight complex and port facility.

For the most part, the city avoided the racial violence that plagued several major cities during the war. But despite having just fought a war for freedom and equality, Memphis remained strictly segregated. In 1947, the American Heritage Foundation sponsored a "Freedom Train" to carry original copies of the Declaration of Independence, the Constitution, and other historically significant documents across the nation to promote national unity and citizenship. The Foundation required the train to be open to all citizens. The scheduled stop in Memphis was canceled rather than allow an integrated crowd to view the documents, based on the belief of then Mayor James Pleasants "that congregating thousands of white people and colored people together . . . would surely lead to trouble and perhaps bloodshed."

Nonetheless, some efforts were made in the direction of racial equity, particularly in city police and fire departments. In 1948, the city hired and trained

The crew of the Memphis Belle, *the first B-17 Flying Fortress to complete 25 missions without casualties, poses in front of the famous plane named for Memphian Margaret Polk, pilot Lieutenant Colonel Robert Morgan's sweetheart.*

nine black policemen. These were the first black policemen in uniform, but not the first African-American men to be employed by law enforcement. In 1919, three African Americans were hired by the police department to work as special plain clothes officers in the black areas, but their tenures lasted less than a week. These new officers were restricted to foot patrol in predominantly black areas of the city, and the men could arrest only members of their own race. Only two of the nine hired in 1948 finished their careers with the police department. Progress was slow; by 1969, black officers comprised only 7.7 percent of the police force. Similarly, the fire department hired an all-black squad in 1955. These men were stationed in the black section of town and commanded by a white lieutenant and captain. Twelve years later, Memphis had more than 1,000 firemen, of whom only 14 were African American. In 1966, these city departments were officially integrated and the numbers began to increase. By the mid-1990s, African Americans comprised 38 percent of police officers and 28 percent of Memphis firemen.

It was in the area of popular culture in the postwar era that the strict separation of black and white began to falter. Memphis music would become a force for change. In 1948, radio station WDIA took the giant leap into black programming. The white-owned station had been struggling with low ratings and weak advertising since its inauguration the previous year. Although blacks constituted nearly half a million of the listeners in the Memphis market, no one took advantage of their potential spending power. Throughout the 1930s, some Memphis radio stations, like WHBQ, had pitched occasional shows to African Americans, playing black music in support of an appeal to buy some product designed specifically for black people. But there were no black disk jockeys nor announcers, and stations feared desertion by mainstream advertisers if they dedicated too much attention to a black audience. With little to lose and a huge black market to gain, WDIA's white owners, Bert Ferguson and John R. Pepper, decided to risk hiring the first African-American radio announcer in the South: Nat D. Williams, a Booker T. Washington history teacher, newspaper columnist, and popular emcee at the Palace Theater on Beale Street. When Williams took the microphone in October 1948 to lead his "Tan Town Jamboree," his gifts as an entertainer were already well-known. He was in charge of the Midnight Rambles, the all-black show for white audiences on Thursday nights, carried live from the Palace Theater on WHBQ. Williams also hosted the legendary Amateur Nights every Tuesday at the Palace.

Memphis municipal law required racial separation and it worked both ways. When famed white folklorist Alan Lomax, who was recording music for the Library of Congress, visited a Beale Street establishment in 1942, he could not buy a meal. A sign on the wall read: "This is a Colored Place. No Whites Served." Whites were invited to Beale Street only one night a week and only to one place. These were known far and wide as the Midnight Rambles, although they were advertised in area posters and newspapers as "Frolic—for White People Only." This was an added showing at midnight of the regular bill, including touring acts like the "Ebony Follies" and "Hot Chocolate," many of them featuring half-clad dancers. Also featured were Beale Street's own Brownskin Models, a lineup of beautiful chorus girls. George W. Lee wrote in *Beale Street: Where the Blues Began*: "On Thursday nights the blues belong to the white people. They come in evening dress in high-powered cars, in overalls and Fords, to see scantily clad brown beauties dancing across the stage in the midnight show at the Palace." Beale Street entrepreneurs knew that whites would pay well to see what they were not allowed to witness in other parts of the city.

The Amateur Night contests, modeled after those at Harlem's famous Apollo Theater, were limited to blacks and on any given night featured dancers, singers, jugglers, comics, and jug bands, all clamoring for the chance to please the tough hometown crowd and win the prize money: $5 for first, $3 for second, and $2 for third place. Nat Williams' side-kick for the show was Rufus Thomas, who maintained that, "If you were black for one night on Beale Street, you would never want to be white again." The amateur show was raucous and high-spirited. Sometimes the worst acts were the hit of the show. If performers were bad enough to get booed by the crowd, they were supposed to leave the stage. Those who stayed got "shot" by the "Lord High Executioner" (usually Rufus) who leaped from the wings and fired blanks at them from his pearl-handled pistol.

This inspired craziness lasted some 30 years at the Palace, and launched some of the biggest names in black entertainment. Most famous was a skinny blues singer from Indianola, Mississippi, named Riley King. He suffered the boos and being shot by the executioner, but kept coming back.

Riley King made his way to WDIA, which featured a wide variety of local musical talent including regional blues stars Little Milton and Junior Parker, gospel groups like the Soul Stirrers, the Songbirds of the South, the Staple Singers, and A.C. Williams and his Teen-Town Singers. King earned a 15-minute segment on Saturday at 5:00 p.m., and became so popular that he soon received his own show. Initially billed as the Beale Street Blues Boy, the nickname was gradually shortened to Blues Boy, then to simply B.B. He made his first recording at the WDIA studios, and continued his radio show for several years while traveling with his band. WDIA became the first all-black radio station in the nation in 1949, grew to a major 50,000-watt station, and held the number two market spot in the mid-South. B.B. King went on to superstardom and currently owns his own club on Beale.

Yet another innovation in radio programming began in 1955 by local record producer Sam Phillips and his wife, Becky, and assistant Marion Keisker. WHER was the first station in the nation with "all-girl" programming. It is difficult today, when so many women work in broadcasting, to comprehend how extraordinary this was. Broadcasting from studios nicknamed the "Doll Den" in the Holiday Inn on South Third, the station featured a female station manager, Dotty Abbott, and eight "disk jockeyettes." WHER remained on the air for 19 years, far longer than other all-girl stations that came later. By the time a new manager changed the format in 1974, women on the radio had ceased to be a novelty.

Phillips was also the guiding force behind the rise of Memphis' premier icon, Elvis Presley, whose fusion of blues, gospel, and country gave birth to a new musical genre that forever changed American music: rock 'n' roll. As John Lennon so famously put it, "Before Elvis, there was nothing." Born dirt-poor in Tupelo, Mississippi, and raised shabby in Lauderdale Courts, Presley was a machinists' mate when he stopped by Phillips' Sun Recording Studio to cut a personal record for his mother. Though his rendition of "My Happiness" was weak and wavering, Phillips thought he had potential. A few months later, Presley's faster-paced version of Arthur "Big Boy" Crudup's blues song, "That's All Right, Mama," launched his incredible career. His sound, combining traditional country music with Delta blues and an urban beat, was uniquely his own.

Among a minority of whites interested in promoting black music, Phillips was fascinated with blues and black culture. He came to Memphis for the specific purpose of recording, as he put it, "genuine, untutored negro music [performed by] negroes with field mud on their boots and patches in their overalls . . . battered instruments and unfettered techniques."[36] Throughout the early 1950s, Phillips recorded the "race music" of Rufus Thomas, who had the first Sun hit with "Bear Cat," Howlin' Wolf, Ike Turner, and many others. Sun also recorded white artists who stretched the limits, including a vacuum cleaner salesman named Johnny

A WHBQ radio microphone dominates this photograph of a famous SUN records quartet.
Left to right: Jerry Lee Lewis, Carl Perkins, Elvis Presley, and Johnny Cash.

Cash singing "Folsom Prison Blues," country singer Carl Perkins' almost-rock tunes "Honey Don't" and "Blue Suede Shoes," and Jerry Lee Lewis' 1957 mega-hits "Whole Lotta Shakin' Goin' On" and "Great Balls of Fire."

Phillips was looking for, he said later, a white man who could sing with the soul of a black man, a liminal artist who could appeal to both sides of segregated music. He believed he found him in Presley. And Presley, for his part, freely acknowledged his debt to black music, much of which he acquired hanging out on Beale Street. Phillips' good friend, disk jockey Dewey Phillips (no relation), played black and white music without distinctions on his nightly "Red, Hot and Blue" program. Dewey was enormously popular, a wild man with a manic sense of humor. He played what he liked and if he liked it a lot, he played it a lot. If he didn't, he would sometimes show his distaste by screeching the needle across the record in mid-song. The day it was released, Dewey played "That's All Right, Mama" 20 times in a row. The response to the record was so great, he sent an assistant to find Presley and bring him to the studio. A very shy Elvis was located at a movie theater, brought to the station, and Dewey coaxed a brief interview by convincing Presley that they were not yet on the air.

Elvis Presley's first concert, to a sold-out crowd at the Overton Park Shell on a hot July night in 1954, launched an amazing career that changed what it meant to be young in America. His flamboyant style, flashy clothes, slicked-back hair, soulful ballads, and erotic postures inspired young girls to scream and their parents to wail. Fame came fast, especially after appearances on the Ed Sullivan and Milton Berle TV programs. In 1955, just days before Presley's twenty-first birthday, Phillips sold his contract to RCA Victor for $40,000, reported in the *Press-Scimitar* as "probably the highest ever paid for a contract release for a country-western recording artist." Phillips received $35,000 and Presley $5,000 out of the deal. Elvis used his first royalty checks to buy a house for his mom and dad at 1034 Audubon Drive. Only three years before, the Presleys were living in public housing; now they lived in one of the nicest upper middle-class neighborhoods in Memphis. Elvis welcomed all fans, signed all autographs. Burdened by too many fans and too many automobiles, his neighbors joined together and offered to buy him out. Seeking refuge from the storm of celebrity, Elvis bought Graceland in 1957, a two-story limestone home with a quasi-Tara-style facade on 13.75 acres for $100,000. No matter how much he traveled, Presley always considered Memphis home, and he returned to Graceland whenever he could. A reporter once asked him what he missed about Memphis and he replied, "everything."

Presley became famous for giving away Cadillacs like boxes of candy. For many years, he also made anonymous donations to countless Memphis charities, and frequently and quietly paid hospital bills, bought homes, and paid off debts for family, friends, and for total strangers.

In all, Elvis Presley recorded 149 songs with a voice of tremendous power and a four-octave range, nearly all of them huge hits. He released 33 mostly formulaic, mostly forgettable films in the 1960s: playboy meets girl, sings, has a few fist fights, sings, gets the girl in the end . . . and sings. His short-lived marriage and incredible career have been well chronicled.

Memphis music captured the nation's imagination and complicated a country's notions of segregating music. First Sun pushed against the barriers. Then in the early 1960s, another recording company came along that again exploited the Memphis hybrid music by blending rhythm and blues, black gospel, and white southern rock. Stax was an interracial organization, founded by brother and sister Jim Stewart and Estelle Axton. Taking its name from the first two letters of their last names, Stax set up shop in an unoccupied movie theater on East McLemore Avenue and College in South Memphis. Located in a black working class neighborhood, Stax opened its doors to blacks and whites alike. The owners were white, the recording artists mostly black and the studio musicians, writers, and arrangers included people of both colors. The father-daughter duo of Rufus and Carla Thomas recorded Stax's first hit, "Cause I Love You." Other artist hits included Otis Reddings' "Sittin' on the Dock of the Bay," the integrated Booker T. and the MGs' "Green Onions," Sam and Dave's "Hold On, I'm Comin'." It also included the black and white duo, Wayne Jackson and Andrew Love, The Memphis Horns. The theme song from the movie *Shaft* became the fastest selling album in Stax history and won an Academy Award for Isaac Hayes for Best Soundtrack. In the 1960s, Stax's major rival was Detroit's Motown Records and disc jockeys referred to Stax as "Soulsville U.S.A," distinguishing the Memphis sound from Motown.

Stax's success spawned smaller labels in Memphis like Hi Records. Artists on their roster included Al Green, the Bill Black Combo, Otis Clay, and Ann Peebles. Willie Mitchell, who began his career in the 1950s with Ace Cannon and Bill Black, took over the recording studio at 1320 South Lauderdale and continued to turn out hit and near-hit records well into the 1990s. By 1973, Memphis was the fourth largest recording center in the world and music recording was the third largest commercial activity in the city. In its 15 years of existence, Stax released 800 singles and 300 full albums, placed over 167 hit songs in the top 100 of the pop charts and 243 hits in the top 100 R&B charts, and won eight Grammies. Stewart and Axton sold the business at the height of its success in 1968. Unfortunately, Stax was financially destroyed by a bad distribution deal with CBS Records and forced into bankruptcy in late 1975. The master tapes were sold at a bankruptcy auction for a fraction of their value; the building was torn down and the artists scattered.

Similar to what was happening in other metropolitan areas, the postwar years in Memphis brought an increasing shift, particularly among middle-class whites, to the suburbs east of the city, abandoning the city center to the minority population. The building of the first suburban mall, Poplar Plaza at Highland and Poplar, was, as it turned out, the beginning of the end for downtown as the prime shopping area of the city. At the center of this new postwar lifestyle was the automobile. Cars

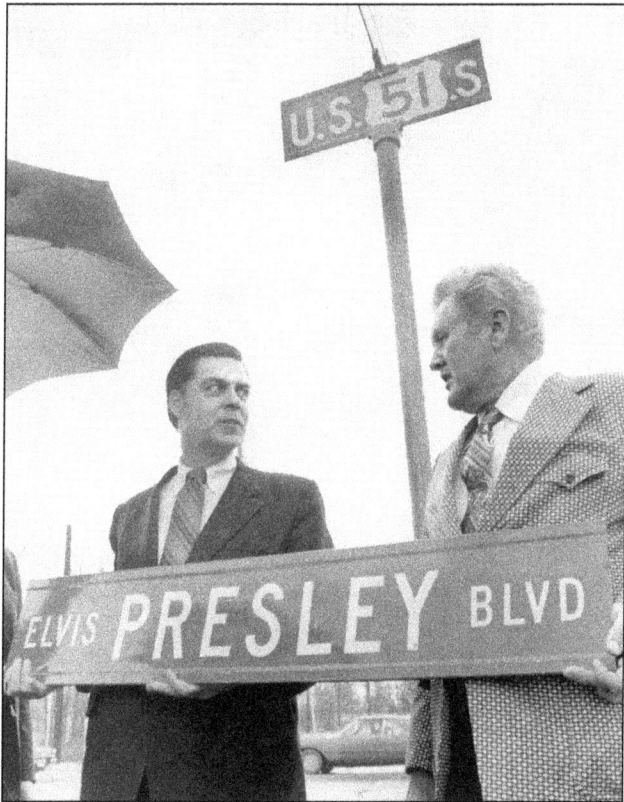

Memphis Mayor Wyeth Chandler and Vernon Presley prepare to change the name of U.S. Highway 51 in honor of the King.

were necessary for living in suburbs and commuting to work and were status-symbols and objects of admiration for the young. Drive-in movies, shopping malls, restaurants, and banks flourished around the city. With money to burn, Memphis youth hung out at hamburger joints like the Pig 'n' Whistle, Fortune's Jungle Garden on Union, or the Tropical Breeze at Poplar and White Station. On weekends they bopped to the Box Tops, the Tribesmen, and the Primitives.

The flip side to all this postwar prosperity and mobility was the increasing distress in the inner city. Urban renewal fervor hit Memphis in the 1950s, initiated by a federal program designed to replace slum housing with new housing, and it lasted into the 1970s. In 1957, the first plan was the Railroad Avenue project, created to eliminate the slums southeast of downtown. Over the years, much of the destroyed housing was not replaced with residences but with businesses and parking lots, or simply left empty, leaving many neighborhoods devastated. During its 20 years of urban renewal, the Memphis Housing Authority was involved in 11 federally approved projects, took over 560 designated acres, and cleared off over 3,000 structures.

By the early 1950s, the Peabody Hotel had fallen victim to a deteriorating urban core. Sold to a Tulsa group in 1953 for $7.5 million, 12 years later the building was

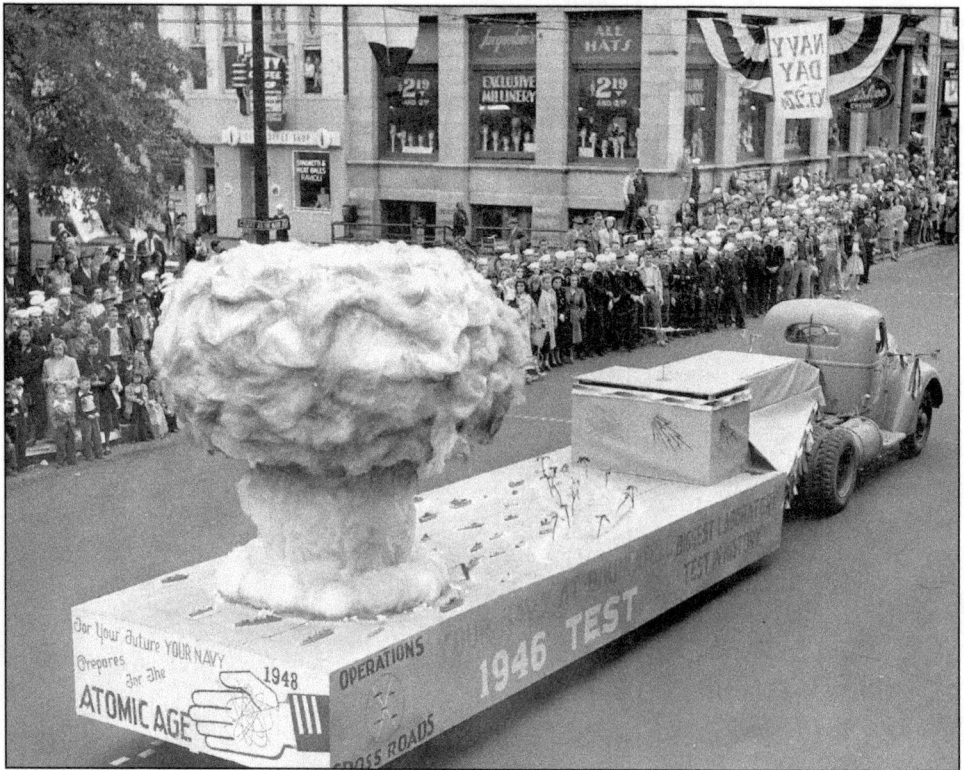

Celebrating America's entry into the atomic age, this float encourages enlistment in the U.S. Navy on Navy Day, October 25, 1948.

128

sold at a foreclosure auction on the Shelby County courthouse steps for $2.3 million to the Snowden family, who had originally built it in 1925. Robert Snowden leased it to the Sheraton Hotel Corporation, who promised to restore the grand hotel. After struggling for ten years, the Peabody was in bankruptcy again in 1975.

Local entrepreneur Kemmons Wilson used his own experiences on a motor trip to revolutionize the travel industry. He took his wife and five children to Washington, D.C. in 1951. Dismayed by the cramped and uncomfortable conditions and the additional $2 per child he was charged at tourist inns along the way, he returned to Memphis determined to build a better motel. His new Holiday Inn, named after a Bing Crosby movie, opened in 1952 at 4941 Summer Avenue. It featured 120 air-conditioned rooms, a restaurant and swimming pool for guests, and children under 12 stayed free in their parents' room. In partnership with Memphis builder Wallace E. Johnson, Wilson built a chain of motels and began franchising them. Soon his distinctive bright green and orange sign became one of the most recognized logos of the twentieth century. Committed to standardization and quality control, Wilson established the Holiday Inn Innkeeping School to train franchisees and employed inspectors to drop in unannounced to grade each motel. After a heart attack in 1979, he sold the chain, but continued his interest in the hospitality business with a series of Wilson World Hotels. "Only work half a day," was his secret for success, he often said. "It doesn't matter which half you work—the first 12 hours or the second 12 hours." Shortly before he died in February 2003, Wilson built the $15 million Kemmons Wilson School of Hospitality and Resort Management on the campus of the University of Memphis.

In 1956, the Army Corp of Engineers made one final stab at obliterating Mud Island. Their plan, which the newspaper reported would "require millions of dollars and perhaps 10 years of time," would "stabilize the Mississippi from Brandywine Chute to Memphis Front [and] encourage the river to reclaim Mud Island." Once again, the Mississippi failed to cooperate. In 1959, a downtown airport was dedicated on the island. Used mostly by shoppers and businessmen looking to get in and out of town quickly, the airport provided a pontoon ferryboat for the short 300-foot trip to the mainland. In 1970, the airport was closed following a bitter fight over a proposed new bridge across the Mississippi that would extend over the north end of the runway. The city replaced the Mud Island Airport with the General DeWitt Spain Airport, north of the Wolf River. Named for a World War II veteran and advisor to the Tennessee Air National Guard, the DeWitt Spain airport continues to operate for the convenience of businessmen.

The 1950s in America and in Memphis were characterized by a growing economy and a sense of vulnerability precipitated by the Cold War with the Soviet Union. By 1949, the Russians had their own atomic bomb and thus Americans had to build a bigger bomb and more of them, while finding ways to protect themselves. Kids in schools practiced duck-and-cover and participated in yearly mock nuclear attack drills involving all levels of the Memphis populace and across the nation. The city installed a system of air raid sirens and people were told to listen for them at Saturday noon to be sure they were working to alert them of a bomb attack. According to a Memphis civil defense manual, "we can be fairly sure of a two-hour warning before the enemy can get here," so citizens should listen for a "five minute steady blast" followed by 1 minute of silence. The plan was simple: get out of the city fast. Memphians were told to abandon their homes, leave their children in the hands of school officials, and proceed in an orderly manner out of the Danger Zone, which was defined as a circle reaching 15 miles from downtown. The assumption was that the bomb would drop downtown rather than on the Defense Depot or the Naval Air Station at Millington or any other of the many tempting targets. In a burst of optimism, the evacuation plan was supposed to assure that the entire population of the city, nearly one-half million at the time, would get out of town during that two hour window.

Those who could not leave town were instructed to go to one of 279 designated civil defense shelters. Unfortunately, these covered only a few areas of the county and had space for only about 143,000 people at full capacity, or about one-fifth of the population. Most of the shelters were stocked with food—"survival crackers and biscuits"—and carbohydrate supplements designed to maintain 700 calories a day. Special sanitation kits, housed in heavy cardboard drums, contained toilet paper, drinking cups, and gloves. The drum, fitted with a special lid and lined with plastic, functioned as a shelter toilet. One of the shelters was at Poplar Plaza, the new shopping center in East Memphis, that had reinforced some of the buildings for this purpose.

Some families decided to build their own shelters, fortifying their basements or scooping out their backyards following plans printed in magazines like *Popular Mechanics*. The Memphis Parade of Homes in the late 1950s included bomb shelters with new homes and several companies sold ready-made bomb shelters that could be dropped in a hole in the ground. The Mid-South Fair in 1961 featured a family living in an all-glass shelter for nine days. None of these humble little shelters could match the one Hoyt Wooten, founder of WREC radio and later television, installed on his estate in Whitehaven. His 13-room underground complex, including sleeping quarters, a recreation room with pool table, and even a morgue, could shelter 52 people for weeks, perhaps months. All of these methods were supposed to make Americans feel safer. And maybe they did. At any rate, they remained unused. In the mid-1970s, more than 23 tons of aging survival crackers from Memphis shelters were shipped to Bangladesh to help feed the starving, and more than a million pounds were fed to livestock at the Shelby County penal farm. Occasionally someone still stumbles upon one of these structures in basements around town, well-preserved time-capsules of the Cold War.

In order to facilitate the rapid evacuation of cities across the nation in the event of an attack, President Eisenhower proposed legislation in 1956 to build an interstate highway system. The Interstate and Defense Highway System would create a 41,000-mile network of superhighways to connect every major city in the

United States. Included in the plans was a stretch of Interstate 40 destined to run straight through the city, bisecting Overton Park, the city's largest green space and home to the Zoo, Brooks Memorial Art Gallery, and the Memphis Art Academy. This decision mobilized a coalition of homeowners and civic leaders who vowed to stop the project and save the park. Calling themselves the Citizens to Protect Overton Park (CPOP), the group collected some 10,000 signatures on petitions and launched letter-writing campaigns, thus beginning a fight that would last 24 years and result in a landmark Supreme Court decision.

Even as the battle was joined, the city began bulldozing hundreds of homes, many of them fine turn-of-the-century residences, that lay in the path of the proposed highway. Like the route itself, the battle divided the city. The Chamber of Commerce, City Council, Downtown Association, the Shelby County Court, the NAACP, and the state of Tennessee all favored the plan as a boost to the downtown economy, improving access from eastern suburbs, and relieving traffic congestion on local streets. Arrayed in opposition were CPOP, the Sierra Club, the Audubon Society, the Council for a Greener Memphis, the Mid-Memphis Improvement Association, and a few others dismayed that the route would take some 26 acres of the park, including a considerable portion of old growth forest.

Mud Island was the site of the downtown airport until 1970, when the De Soto Bridge was built. The airport's slogan: "You are strictly uptown when you land downtown."

With legal assistance from the Sierra Club, CPOP launched a series of lawsuits and injunctions that went all the way to the Supreme Court. *Citizens to Preserve Overton Park, Incorporated v. Volpe* (the Secretary of Transportation) was decided in 1973 in CPOP's favor. Memphis became the only spot on the map where I-40 stops. This impasse was later resolved by giving the I-40 designation to the northern loop on the expressway. In the late 1990s, a new generation of homes began to fill in the Overton Park corridor.

A major Memphis institution arose at the confluence of the crosstown interstates. St. Jude Children's Research Hospital opened in 1962, devoted to research and treating serious childhood diseases. Legend has it that entertainer Danny Thomas was down to his last $7 when he knelt before a statue of St. Jude of Thaddeus, patron saint of hopeless causes, seeking direction in his life and promising a shrine. Thomas went on to be very successful with a TV series called "Make Room for Daddy" and the shrine became St. Jude's. Children with serious diseases are never turned away, regardless of their ability to pay. Costs not covered by insurance are absorbed by ALSAC (the American Lebanese Syrian Associated Charities), the fund-raising arm of the hospital. Research by St. Jude's has had a dramatic effect on the cure rate for acute lymphoblastic leukemia, the most common pediatric cancer. Forty years ago it was four percent; in 2000, the cure rate is 80 percent. Today, St. Jude's is known for its research in gene therapy, bone marrow transplants, and chemotherapy. Dr. Peter Doherty of St. Jude's was awarded the 1996 Nobel Prize for Medicine for his work on T-cell recognition and cell-mediating therapy. Danny Thomas died in 1991, having seen his dream celebrate its nineteenth anniversary. He and his wife are buried in the family crypt on the grounds of the hospital.

One of the most important business transactions in the city's history took place in 1972 when Fred Smith founded Federal Express Corporation at Memphis International Airport. Though his business plan for an air cargo company earned him a C at Yale, Smith was convinced there was a market for time-sensitive shipments. Beginning with 14 small aircraft, the company initially serviced 25 American cities. By November 1988, package volume reached the one million mark. Now the world's largest express transportation system, Fed Ex employs approximately 30,000 Memphians, serves more than 200 countries, handles 3.3 million packages and documents every night, and has made Memphis the busiest cargo airport in the nation.

13. THE STRUGGLE FOR POWER

African Americans in Memphis and elsewhere returned home from the war determined to find equality in American society. Black leadership recognized that political organizing was the key to claiming some measure of equity. Several groups, including the Ministers and Citizens League, an interdenominational group of black ministers, began serious efforts to increase voter registration and education. In 1951, Dr. J.E. Walker, founder and head of the Universal Life Insurance Company, offered himself as a candidate for the Memphis Board of Education. He was the only candidate, black or white, to challenge the Crump slate that year. Walker won 7,483 votes while each of the four white candidates got more than 21,000. Less than 20,000 blacks were registered to vote that year. Following this defeat and the elimination of the poll tax in 1954, drives in the black community pushed registration to 60 percent of eligible voters. As blacks struggled for the right to vote across the South during the Civil Rights movement, black Memphians were already registered at roughly the same rate as white Memphians. This voting bloc provided political leverage in an arena where the voting age population was approximately 34 percent black. As long as they could harness that bloc, the black leadership was able to negotiate concessions from a white leadership needing their support.

A handful of African Americans achieved political office in the 1960s and ultimately succeeded in altering the city charter to ensure more equitable representation. Two were elected to the state legislature, the first since the late nineteenth century: A.W. Willis to the Tennessee House of Representatives and Russell Sugarmon, Jr. to the Tennessee Senate. In 1965, Governor Frank G. Clement appointed attorney Benjamin Hooks to the judgeship of the new Criminal Court Division IV, making him the first African American to hold such a post in Tennessee since Reconstruction. This same leadership campaigned for a change in the structure of city government. All commissioners were then elected at large, ensuring white domination. The new charter, which was finally adopted in 1967, called for a strong mayor executive and a 13-member council, of which seven members would represent specific districts of the city. This change to district voting ensured a measure of power over city government that had been unavailable to blacks for over 50 years, and by 1996 African Americans held a majority on the City Council with seven members.

Benjamin Hooks (shown here with wife Frances Dancy Hooks) became the first black criminal court judge in Tennessee in 1965; he later served on the Federal Communications Commission and served as Executive Director of the National Association for the Advancement of Colored People from 1976 to 1992.

Nineteen fifty-four was a pivotal year in Memphis. Edward Hull "Boss" Crump died, and the U.S. Supreme Court ruled in *Brown v. the Board of Education of Topeka, Kansas* that separate but equal was unlawful and called for desegregation "with all deliberate speed." The brief and simple ruling was the judicial equivalent of the shot heard round the world. Although the decision referred directly only to school segregation, in striking down the "separate but equal" doctrine the Supreme Court implied that all legal segregation was unconstitutional. Southern whites were outraged, and they dubbed May 17 as "Black Monday." Nineteen Southern senators and 77 Southern representatives, including Memphis' Representative Clifford H. Davis, issued the "Southern Manifesto" condemning the Court decision as a usurpation of state powers, a decision bent upon "destroying the amicable relations between the white and Negro races that have been created through ninety years of patient effort by the good people of both races." The Manifesto bound the signers to "use all lawful means to bring about a reversal of this decision . . . and to prevent the use of force in its implementation." Among Southern senators, only Lyndon Johnson of Texas and the two Tennessee senators, Estes Kefauver and Albert Gore, refused to sign. Southern governors called for "massive resistance" to school integration. The Ku Klux Klan was revived along with a host of new groups such as the National Association for the Advancement of White People, and a quarter million Southerners joined local White Citizens' Councils to defend segregation. In Memphis a new organization, calling themselves Citizens for Progress, declared for a racial status quo: "Keep Memphis Down in Dixie" was their slogan. And in 1955, one year after the Brown decision rendered separate schools unconstitutional, the Memphis City School Board built Lester High School for blacks, less than a mile from all-white East High. It was shaping up to be a long fight.

The Memphis NAACP accepted the challenge, first attacking segregation in a number of tax-supported public institutions with a flurry of suits filed in 1960. The targets were the city's libraries, parks, golf courses, playgrounds, auditoriums, fairgrounds, and swimming pools. After the library was desegregated under court order, the NAACP was back in court to get "colored" and "white" restroom and drinking fountain signs removed. Three years of legal action, boycotts, weekly marches, sit-ins, and hundreds of arrests resulted in city buses, downtown lunch counters, the public library, the Pink Palace, Overton Park and Zoo, the Brooks Art Gallery, movie theaters, and restaurants being opened to African Americans. Still, Memphis integration avoided much of the animosity and violence found in other parts of the South. This could be at least partially attributable to the Memphis Committee on Community Relations (MCCR) as an unofficial interracial group of business, civic, and religious leaders who worked behind the scenes with a plan for moderate, gradual, and calm desegregation. Well before the passage of the National Civil Rights Act of 1964, Memphis dismantled many of the barriers to full participation in public life. The remaining battles however would be fought over the schools, and these would drag on well into the 1970s.

First came a challenge at the college level. In 1955, five black Memphis students, including Maxine Carr (later Smith), who held a Master's degree from Middlebury College in Vermont, and Miriam DeCosta Sugarmon, a Phi Beta Kappa from Wellesley, were refused admittance to Memphis State College as unqualified for graduate school. The group sought a federal injunction against the state board of education. The board responded with a five-year plan to desegregate, beginning with graduate students and descending to a lower grade each year. This satisfied the court and the injunction was denied. On appeal, the U.S. Supreme Court in 1957 found the plan unacceptable, ruling that Tennessee colleges must admit qualified black students in accordance with the equal protection clause of the 14th Amendment. In 1959, shortly after Memphis State College achieved university status, integration began with the enrollment of eight black students, five women and three men. The Memphis State Eight faced hostile crowds waving Confederate battle flags and "Civil Rights for Whites" signs. They had police escorts to classes, were denied access to the school cafeteria and the student center, and were required to leave the campus by noon. But change had begun and would not be stopped.

Six years after the Brown decision, a group of attorneys, including Benjamin Hooks and Thurgood Marshall, filed a lawsuit, *Northcross v. Memphis Board of Education*, for total and immediate desegregation of all city schools. It would be 20 years before the final decision in this case and the implementation of an acceptable plan for a unitary school system. In their answer to the suit, the board denied that they were operating a compulsory biracial school system. If segregation existed, said the board, it was strictly voluntary owing to the desire of members of one race to associate and attend school with members of the same race. The local judge agreed and found for the defendants. The following year, the decision was reversed by a higher court. That fall, 13 African-American first-graders were admitted to four all-white schools under massive police protection and a news blackout. Unlike in many other states, which fought the decision with violence and a venomous outflow of racial hatred, Memphis was orderly and without fanfare. The agreement was for another grade to be integrated each year, yet the pace was glacially slow. In 1962, black enrollment at previously all-white schools stood at 53. An order of the U.S. Sixth Circuit Court of Appeals in 1964 attempted to accelerate the process, mandating that all junior high schools must be integrated by the start of the 1965–1966 fall term, and all high schools the following year. The order was largely ignored.

The Memphis State Eight desegregated Memphis State University in 1959. They are, from left to right: (front row) Bertha Rogers, LaVerne Kneeland, Rosie Blakney, Sammie Burnett, and Luther McClellan; (back row) John Simpson, Eleanor Gandy, and Ralph Prater.

By the late 1960s, the turmoil of the civil rights movement had been going on for over ten years, but by and large Memphis had avoided the worst of the hot summers of violence that plagued many major cities. Whites believed they had been most cooperative and race relations were moving along quite nicely. The *Press-Scimitar* in March 1968 claimed Memphis was "the city with the best race relations in the nation."[37] But for blacks, there had been too little progress and nothing had been done to address the deeply rooted problems of poverty and prejudice. These conflicting perceptions were played out in the political arena where the Democrats were perceived as the party of civil rights and the Republican Party emerged as the party of white resistance. The divergence of black and white interests meant an end to coalition and compromise.

Mayor Henry Loeb was elected by a solid white vote in 1967 against moderates and reformers, while the change in the city's charter resulted in three African Americans serving on the city council. Loeb's new administration had barely moved into their offices when he was faced with a labor problem that quickly escalated into a civil rights problem. Memphis' sanitation workers went on strike on February 28, pressing for an increase in the pay that still left them eligible for welfare, a handful of basic benefits like health care, an end to differential treatment by race, and recognition of their union (The American Federation of State, County and Municipal Employees [AFSCME] local number 1733). The precipitating incident was when rain canceled a workday and 22 sewer and drain workers received pay for only two hours while their white supervisors collected full pay. It then accelerated when two black workers were accidentally crushed to death in a garbage compactor and their widows received no insurance benefits. Mayor Loeb insisted public employees were not permitted to strike, therefore the strike was illegal and he refused to negotiate. The mayor's hard line and the hostile reaction to it by the white community shifted a labor dispute into a racial confrontation. The garbage men became a symbol of protest against economic and racial injustice for the entire black community. Daily marches and sit-ins at City Hall led to increasingly tense confrontations. The Reverend Martin Luther King, Jr., who had recently been turning his civil rights efforts toward economic issues and preparing to launch an interracial "poor people's campaign," came to Memphis. Convinced the strike in Memphis was the embodiment of his commitment to economic justice, King held a rally on March 18, agreeing to return again to lead a mass march in support of the strikers.

On March 28, the hundreds of black men carrying signs reading "I Am a Man" gathered around King at Clayborn African Episcopal Methodist Temple on Hernando. The route of the march would take them down Beale Street to Main and east to City Hall. Before they left Beale Street, though, the march turned violent. Windows along the route were smashed by youthful protesters impatient with nonviolent demonstrations, calling themselves The Invaders. The police response left one dead, 62 injured, and more than 300 arrested. The peaceful demonstration had become a riot. King was hustled from harm's way as soon as the violence started but the damage to his reputation as a non-violent leader was

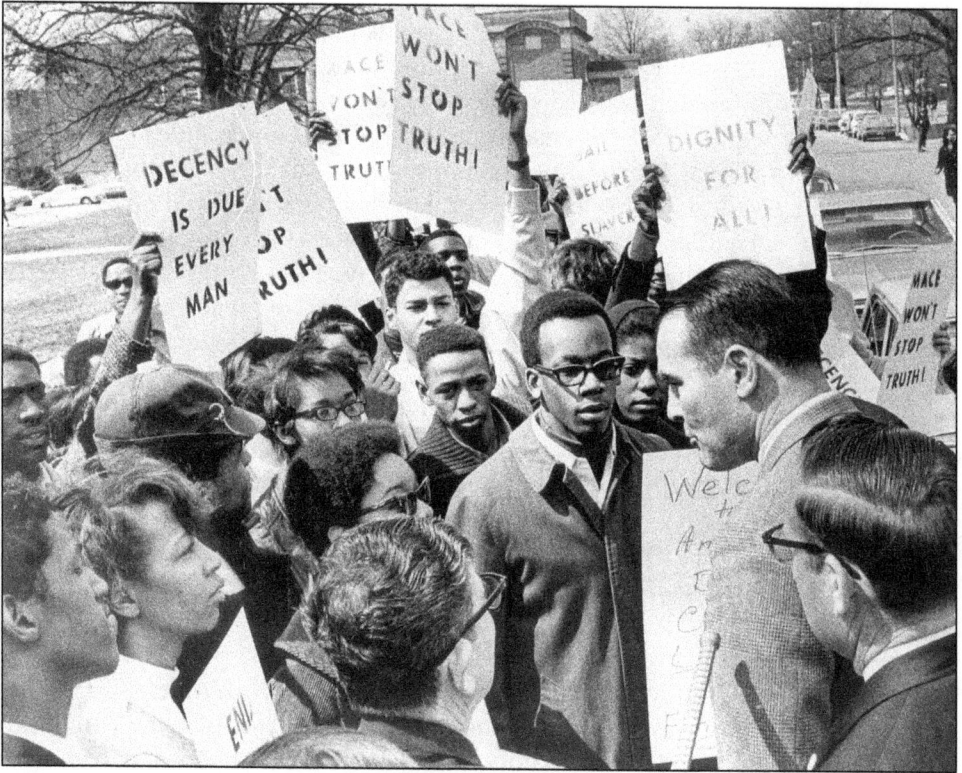

Mayor Henry Loeb confronts demonstrators seeking social justice for African Americans during tense times in Memphis in March 1968.

in shambles. Within the movement, as well as in Memphis, calls for black power were forcing a referendum on his leadership. With little choice, King vowed to return to Memphis to lead a non-violent march in April.

On the night of April 3, in the midst of a violent thunderstorm, King spoke to a mass meeting about having been to the mountaintop and seeing the promised land. The following evening, as King was preparing for another mass march, he was assassinated as he stood on the balcony outside Room 306 of the Lorraine Motel. A single rifle shot fired from the bathroom of a boarding house across the street shattered King's jaw and he died within minutes. A drifter from Texas, James Earl Ray, was arrested for the killing and served out a life sentence at Middle Tennessee's Brushy Mountain State Prison.

In the aftermath of the assassination, cities across the nation exploded in racial violence: Detroit, Chicago, New York, Pittsburgh, Boston, Baltimore, and Washington, D.C.—but not Memphis. Mayor Loeb imposed a curfew and called out 4,000 National Guardsmen to secure the divided city but, despite scattered incidents of looting and burning, the expected conflagration did not happen. Much of the credit for the city's relative peace remains with the majority of the black community that dealt with their anger in the way Dr. King had instructed and the handful of black-white coalitions like Memphis Cares and the Memphis Search for Meaning Committee. Four days after the death of her husband, Coretta Scott King and her children led a completely silent march of some 40,000 people from across the nation through the streets of Memphis.

On April 16 and after 65 bitter days, the city settled with the sanitation workers, recognized their union, and agreed to a modest raise. But great damage had been done to the city's race relations and its national reputation. Everyone knew Memphis was the place where they killed Dr. King. *Time* magazine reported: "The proximate cause of his death was, ironically, a minor labor dispute in a Southern backwater; the two-month-old strike of 1,300 predominantly Negro garbage collectors in the decaying Mississippi river town of Memphis."

Even before the sanitation strike, the central city had been largely deserted by white Memphians heading east, taking retail establishments, businesses, and jobs with them. Plans formulated by the Memphis Housing Authority in 1966 to convert Beale Street into a city centerpiece with high-rise apartments and a commercial mall, and promises to build a new auditorium in Church Park, were abandoned in the wake of the assassination. Within a few weeks, as racial tensions were at their peak, the city's urban renewal projects dubbed Beale Street I and Beale Street II, leveled every building north and south of Beale and along one block of Beale itself. Four-hundred seventy-four buildings were demolished, displacing more than 300 families, reducing the resident population to zero, and leaving behind a score of empty lots and a thin commercial district between Second and Fourth Avenues.

One of the most difficult tasks of the civil rights era remained unresolved in Memphis. At the beginning of the 1968–1969 school year, 35 city schools remained all white, 50 all black. Over 71 percent of black students attended all-black schools. Minority leaders staged a series of Black Monday protest marches and launched student boycotts of schools and economic boycotts of city merchants. After the U.S. Supreme Court ruled that busing was an appropriate

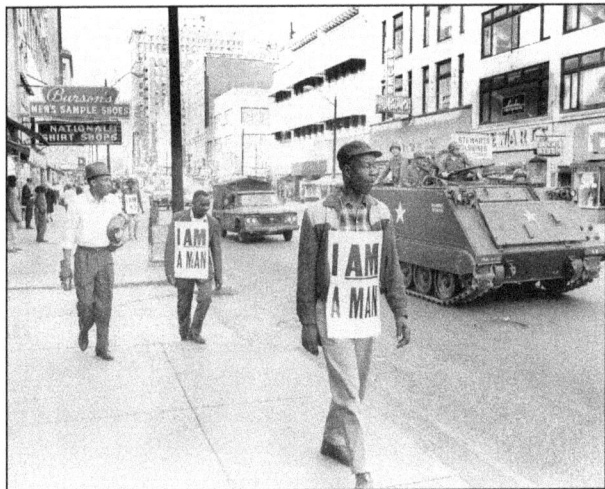

Strikers did not carry signs asking for union recognition or civil rights. Each wore a sign stating simply, "I Am a Man." Here military equipment and troops patrol Memphis streets in an attempt to quell possible violence.

means to integrate schools, U.S. District Judge Robert M. McRae ruled that Memphis could no longer maintain a system of single-race schools. He issued desegregation order Plan A, calling for busing 13,000 students of the system's 145,581 pupils to achieve racial balance. When this was rejected by the courts as insufficient, Plan Z called for busing nearly 40,000 students. The orders were met with a firestorm of protests. White parents picketed public schools and enrolled their children in private schools. Many moved out of the city where their children could enroll in mostly white county schools. Over 28,000 white students left the Memphis City School System. Judge McRae received death threats; armed guards were posted outside his courtroom and U.S. marshals guarded his home.

Anti-busing forces included ten members of the city council withholding funds to purchase gasoline for school buses and then-Mayor Wyeth Chandler, who urged a boycott by white students, stating, "I cannot and will not urge any parent to send his child into a ghetto school."[38] Citizens Against Busing (CAB) vowed to resist, staging a mock funeral, complete with hearse and casket, "for the death of neighborhood schools," and buried a school bus, a stunt earning them national publicity. Church-affiliated "white flight" academies mushroomed in eastern Shelby County and northern Mississippi, filling church buildings once used only on Sundays and Wednesday evenings. By 1975, Memphis had one of the nation's largest private school enrollments: 35,000 students in 90 private schools. In the process, Memphis City Schools remained segregated. In the mid 1990s, the black/white ratio in the city schools was 82 percent black, 18 percent white. This mirrored the county school ratio of 18 percent white, 80 percent black, and 2 percent other. Most private schools, with the notable exception of Memphis Catholic, remain overwhelmingly white.

In 1974, Harold Ford became the first black Tennessean elected to Congress, defeating four-term incumbent Dan Kuykendall for the Ninth District seat and signaling a significant change in black political power in Memphis. Ford developed a very effective political operation based upon constituent service. "Harold delivers" was his slogan, and his deliveries included job training programs, food at Christmas, a sample ballot to assist his supporters in the voting booth, and help through the maze of federal and local bureaucracies. Ford served in Congress from 1974 to 1996. In 1987, he was indicted for conspiracy and bank fraud; it would be six years of mistrials and delays before he was finally acquitted in 1993. Ford's corps of loyal supporters did not desert him. Indeed, they were key to electing his son, Harold Ford, Jr., to succeed him to Congress in 1996.

In the 1980s, the number of black voters surpassed white voters in Memphis by a 50–49 percent margin, at least partly attributable to the out-migration of whites to the suburbs of eastern Shelby County. Despite some deep divisions within the black community, voters began to elect more African Americans, including women, to city positions. Minerva Johnican was elected in 1983 to an at-large council seat, and in 1990 Earnestine Hunt won a city court position.

In 1991, Memphis' first black Memphis City Schools superintendent, Dr. W.W. "Willie" Herenton, defeated incumbent Mayor Richard Hackett in one of the

Citizens Against Busing bury a school bus in a symbolic act of defiance. The sign reads: "Here lies a school bus. No mourning for us. No more fuming. No more fussing. May this be the end of busing."

closest elections in history, winning with only 142 votes out of a quarter million cast. Herenton took over half of one of the only systems in the country that includes both a city mayor and city council, and a county mayor and county commission. In the same year, the city council was nearly evenly divided, with whites holding a 7–6 majority, while blacks held the majority of school board seats. As a result of suits brought under the 1965 Voting Rights Act, the city council changed from 13 members, 6 of whom were elected at large, to a 9-member single-district formula that would lead to a black majority. The county commission went from 11 to 13 members selected in multi-member districts. The county mayor, Jim Rout, served with a majority white county commission and school board. While racial polarization continued to characterize city and county politics, Mayor Herenton was reelected in 1995, and again in 1999, with broad support from both the black and white community. In 2002, attorney and head of the Public Defenders Office A.C. Wharton was elected Shelby County's first black mayor, signaling a change in the racial polarization of Memphis politics.

Herenton focused his administration on downtown development, an effort that would begin to bear fruit in the late 1990s and into the new century, as Memphis experienced a revival that has become a model for the nation. One early piece of the renewal was coming to terms with the painful assassination of Dr. Martin Luther King, Jr. and its bitter aftermath. The Lorraine Motel, a modest business in 1968, had seriously declined. By 1982, it was a foreclosed property and slated for demolition. A group of concerned citizens formed the Martin Luther King Memorial Foundation to save the building as a shrine to the fallen leader. The Lorraine was reborn as the National Civil Rights Museum in 1991 with 16 galleries to tell the story of the African-American freedom struggle from the 1600s until the murder of Dr. King in 1968. A plaque outside Room 306 quotes Genesis: "They said one to another, behold here cometh the Dreamer. Let us slay him and we shall see what becomes of his dreams." An $11 million expansion connecting the Lorraine with the Main Street rooming house from which the fatal shot was fired was completed in September 2002. This new wing, entitled "Exploring the Legacy," examines ways in which the American Civil Rights Movement was a prototype for human rights movements throughout the world.

After the assassination, African Americans hoped to preserve the Lorraine Motel as a shrine for Dr. King. Note the wreath on the door and the protective glass around the balcony where he fell. In 1991, the National Civil Rights Museum opened within the shell of the old motel.

14. RENAISSANCE

Confronted with a deserted city center and scores of empty lots, Memphians in the 1970s moved to preserve what remained and to engage the renewal side of urban renewal, marking a turning point in the long-term deterioration or abandonment of historical structures. This preservation movement involved a host of formal and informal organizations. Established in 1975, the Memphis Landmarks Commission, a nine-member board appointed by the mayor to preserve the historical integrity of the city, was the chief force behind the preservation of the Cotton Row Historic District, saving historic cotton mercantile houses along Front Street. The Center City Commission, a 20-member board, was chartered in 1977 to direct the comprehensive redevelopment of the central business district and act as an official partner between local government and private business in downtown revitalization.

Memphis Heritage, Incorporated (MHI), a non-profit group of volunteers, was organized to save, improve, reuse, and maintain architecturally and historically significant buildings and neighborhoods. With MHI's active involvement in surveying and certifying city structures, Memphis became number six in the nation in buildings and neighborhoods listed in the National Register of Historic Places. Such listing provides special tax benefits for rehabilitation and adaptive reuse of historic structures. MHI offers unique financial incentives for adaptive reuse of historic buildings: developers donate the facade to MHI in exchange for a tax deduction; the non-profit thereby retains responsibility for insuring that the building's historical integrity is preserved.

Many historic buildings in downtown Memphis have been converted to apartments or combinations of retail and living space, including the Exchange Building, the Commerce Title Building, and the Shrine Building, among many others along Cotton Row and the riverfront. The 15-story Tennessee Trust Building converted to a luxury hotel called The Madison, which opened in 2001. Along the South Main Street Historic District, a host of old warehouses and commercial buildings have been transformed into artists' studios, art galleries, specialty restaurants, and upscale shops on the street level, with loft apartments above. Anchoring the south end of Main Street is Central Station, designed in 1914 by Daniel Burnham. The once-bustling Amtrak depot had fallen into a state

Peabody Place, a shopping and entertainment complex in the heart of downtown, opened a block from Beale and beside the historic Peabody Hotel.

of decay and become a source of embarrassment to the city. A partnership with MHI to obtain historic tax credits made renovation a viable option and in 1999, the station reopened as an intermodal transportation hub with trains, buses, and trolleys, as well as a mix of commercial space and apartments. The old Power House behind Central Station has been transformed into exhibition space by the non-profit Delta Axis.

Historic preservation was not the exclusive province of formal organizations and developers. Memphians joined neighborhood associations and rallied to save a number of showplace homes built on what was then the outskirts of the city. Fourteen historic structures in the Adams-Jefferson Street area, now known as Victorian Village, were restored, including three mansions along Adams Avenue that remain museums to a long-vanished way of life. Neighborhood preservation groups, like those in Annesdale Park, Central Gardens, Cooper-Young, and Vollintine-Evergreen, concentrated their efforts on stabilizing historic but also thriving contemporary neighborhoods. The Downtown Neighborhood Association chose a similar mission as residents began to return to the central city. Drawn by riverfront views and urban living, nearly 2,000 people lived downtown by the end of the 1980s; Memphis was hailed as a boomtown by *Fortune* magazine in 1987.

The revival of downtown Memphis started with the renovation of the "Grand Old Lady" at Union and Second: the Peabody Hotel. In July 1975, developer Jack Belz purchased the derelict hotel for $75,000 and began a $24 million renovation. The magnificent hotel reopened six years later and sparked the investment that would make Memphis a vibrant city once again. Belz later purchased eight city blocks to create Peabody Place, a complex of offices, retail space, restaurants, a movie theater, and the rehabilitation of the old Gayoso Hotel into high-end condominiums.

At the north end of downtown, city planners in the 1970s began to pour money into convention facilities. The Cook Convention Center opened in 1974 adjacent to the old Ellis Auditorium. That same year, the city transformed 4,000 feet of Main Street into a pedestrian corridor called Mid-America Mall in an effort to lure small businesses and shoppers there and to downtown. A fleet of vintage trolleys resumed carrying Memphians gracefully down the Mid-America Mall and around downtown in 1993.

With new development and attractions for tourists downtown, the city once again confronted the question of what to do with Mud Island. The possibilities for developing this unwanted piece of real estate were altered by the construction of a new six-lane bridge linking Interstate 40 across the Mississippi River. To solve the problem of navigation under the bridge, the U.S. Army Corps of Engineers cut a new channel down one side of Mud Island and deposited the dirt on top of the remaining portion. This raised the island a full 20 feet, well above flood stage, halting the seasonal flooding that plagued the island since its creation.

The De Soto Bridge is nearing completion in this picture taken in 1972. Mud Island and the downtown airport are in the foreground. In 1986, 2,000 lights strung along the bridge created a giant M, a spectacular landmark for the city.

145

In 1973, the Hernando de Soto bridge opened, and the following year, architect Roy Harrover took on the task of developing Mud Island. The $7 million concept became a $63 million reality, featuring a museum dedicated to the history of the river, containing a full-scale replica of an 1870s steamboat, a 4,300 seat amphitheater with the downtown skyline for a backdrop, and a shiny new monorail to carry visitors across the river. The complex's centerpiece is a 2,000-foot flowing scale model of the Mississippi River, tracing the lower 1,000 miles of the crooked waterway that rises and falls with the river level. Scaled 30 inches to the mile, one can walk from Cairo, Illinois, to the Gulf of Mexico swimming pool in minutes. Mayors from 20 cities along the Mississippi brought river water from their doorsteps to pour into the scale model at the park's opening on July 4, 1982. The celebration also included a re-enactment of the Battle of Memphis, a concert by the Preservation Hall Jazz Band from New Orleans, and a performance of Hal Holbrooke's "Mark Twain Tonight."

Unfortunately, Mud Island never quite lived up to its promise of a major tourist destination. Perhaps this is because the city's conception of the project differed from the architect's from the beginning. Harrover thought Mud Island should be

Mud Island's 2,000-foot long flowing scale model of the Mississippi River, tracing every curve and every town and bridge in topographic detail, rises and falls with the river level.

146

a public park; the city wanted it to pay its own way, even make money for the city. The result was a lovely park that fell short of being an exciting tourist attraction, but one made too expensive to enjoy by the locals.

Two attractions developed in the 1980s would prove more significant in attracting tourist dollars: Graceland and the transformation of Beale Street. The whole nation was stunned by the news of Elvis Presley's death on August 16, 1977, at the age of 42. The county medical examiner identified the cause of death as coronary arrhythmia, apparently brought on by his serious addiction to a cornucopia of prescription drugs. Following a funeral ceremony at Graceland, he was buried at Forest Hill Cemetery. Within a few days, under serious concerns about his ability to rest in peace in the public cemetery, Elvis' body was disinterred and brought home for burial at Graceland.

At the time he died, Graceland was losing over half a million dollars a year in maintenance and taxes. To stem the flow, Priscilla Presley decided to open the mansion to the public and hired Jack Soden, a Kansas City investment counselor, as CEO of Elvis Presley Enterprises to manage Graceland and license Elvis-related products and ventures. Graceland opened for tours on June 7, 1982, and has become a veritable shrine for millions of fans from around the world. Annually, 600,000 visitors from every state and nearly every foreign country come to tour Graceland's 1970s decor of white wall-to-wall carpeting, gilded piano, mirrored hallways, and the famous jungle room with trickling waterfall and Polynesian-primitive furnishings.

Every year on the anniversary of his death, fans converge on Memphis for "Elvis Week" festivities featuring tribute artists (the preferred term for Elvis impersonators), parades, and fireworks, capped by an all-night candlelight vigil in the street outside the mansion. Elvis sightings continue to be reported around the world and kids too young to remember the King arrive to worship at the shrine. Over 100,000 fans came for the 25th anniversary of his death in 2002. Graceland and the Elvis phenomena transformed the tourist industry in Memphis, having an economic impact on the city estimated at over $150 million a year.

After completion of the last phase of urban renewal in the late 1970s, little remained of the once vibrant Beale Street. The remaining African-American businesses were forced out through condemnation as the city bought almost all properties along three blocks of Beale. Only two establishments, Schwab's and Hudkins Hardware, were still open for business. Only Schwab's, in continuous operation since 1876, has survived. The store has never modernized. Its rectangular display islands are heaped with curios, clothing, household goods, hardware, mechanical toys, and other assorted merchandise. The store's slogan is "If you can't find it at Schwab's, you probably don't need it."

Beale Street Management took on redeveloping the street as a tourist destination in 1982. Few buildings remained intact. A heroic effort was made to save the Gallina Exchange—built in 1891—a three-story building with elegant brick work, arches of brick framing its third-story windows, and a terra-cotta cornice at the top. Once the grandest structure on Beale, all that remains is the facade shored up with six steel girders; the building was so badly damaged it could not be salvaged. City building codes prevent its renovation because it sits atop the Gayoso Bayou. The area behind the facade is an open-air bar and entertainment area, part of Silky O' Sullivan's operation next door.

Two important laws helped transform Beale into an entertainment district: one allowing patrons to purchase alcoholic beverages between Second and Fourth on Beale and legally carry it in the street, and the other permitting Beale establishments to sell liquor until 5:00 a.m. and stay open on Sunday. Gradually, tourist-oriented restaurants, bars, and entertainment venues opened along the three-block strip and by the end of the 1990s, Beale Street offered: B.B. King's, Willie Mitchell's Rum Boogie, The New Daisy Theater, the Hard Rock Café, Elvis Presley's Memphis (in the old Lansky's Clothing Store where Elvis bought his famous duds), Alfred's, Blues City Café, Silky O'Sullivan's, King's Palace, and the Black Diamond. Taking over a section of empty lots to the south of Beale, the Gibson Guitar Corporation opened a factory and the superb Rock 'n' Soul Museum in 2002, a collaboration with the Smithsonian Institution that traces the journey from blues and gospel to rock 'n' roll and soul.

Memphis' premier soul venue, Stax, had been closed since 1975 and the building was demolished in 1989; nothing was left but a state historical marker at the site on McLemore and College—but the dream lived on. Twenty-five years later, Stax began a resurrection. Soulsville, a non-profit corporation, headed by Ms. Deanie Parker, the second Stax employee hired in 1964, initiated the $20 million Soulsville Revitalization Project with a "Ground Shakin', Ground Breakin' " for a Stax Museum of American Soul Music and Stax Music Academy and Performing Arts Center. Located on the 4-acre site of the original Stax Studio, in the heart of a neglected neighborhood, the project inspired others, including a new Hope VI housing development, the LeMoyne-Owen College Community Development Corporation, and the McLemore Development Project, to rehabilitate existing residences and attract new housing and businesses to the area. The Music Academy, aimed at using music as a tool to change the lives of urban youth, opened in July 2002; the museum held its grand opening May 1, 2003, with a "Soul Comes Home" concert by many of the original artists.

At the west end of the Beale entertainment district is the magnificently renovated Orpheum Theater. Serving as a Malco movie theater from 1940 to 1976, it was in the path of urban renewal when the Memphis Development Foundation bought it in 1977. Five years later, in 1982, they closed the theater on Christmas to begin a $5 million renovation to restore it to its former glory. After a grand reopening in 1984 and further upgrading in the 1990s to allow major Broadway productions, the Orpheum now presents two seasons of Broadway shows, hosts Ballet Memphis and Opera Memphis, and welcomes a broad array of entertainers.

Another entertainment, as well as educational, venue opened in the 1980s. Community leader Honey Scheidt encouraged then-mayor Richard Hackett to bring Ramesses the Great, an exhibit from the Egyptian Museum in Cairo, to downtown Memphis in 1987. The exhibition opened in the Cook Convention

Center and featured 74 Egyptian antiquities, including a colossal 47-ton, 25-foot-tall statue of Ramesses the Great discovered at the site of ancient Memphis. The exhibition drew 675,000 visitors. Following this success, Wonders: the Memphis International Cultural Series was founded in 1989 to provide Memphians with a series of large-scale cultural exhibitions in order "to witness the splendors, the marvels, the wonders of the world." A not-for-profit organization, Wonders has produced nine of the most comprehensive and elaborate cultural exhibitions in the world: Catherine the Great (1991), Splendors of the Ottoman Sultans (1992), The Etruscans (1992), Napoleon (1993), Imperial Tombs of China (1995), Titanic (1997), Ancestors of the Incas (1998), World War II Through Russian Eyes (1999), and Eternal Egypt: Masterworks from the British Museum (2001). They all averaged over 650,000 visitors.

The Egyptian theme was a natural for Memphis. A large-scale replica of a pyramid was built to represent Memphis at the 1897 Tennessee Centennial Exposition, and the pyramid symbol was popular for Memphis products, company names, and awards. Over the years, there was talk of building a pyramid by the riverside as a signature landmark of the city. A serious proposal for a golden glass pyramid was put forward in the 1970s, but never developed. In the 1980s, influential businessmen backed the idea of a pyramid-shaped arena and convinced

The brightly lit AutoZone Park, home to the Memphis Redbirds, glows on opening night, April 1, 2000. The Redbirds defeated the St. Louis Cardinals 10–6.

149

the city and county governments to fund it. As the project got underway, a Denver developer named Sidney Shlenker came to town promising to rejuvenate Mud Island and finance several private development projects to complement the arena, including a Hard Rock Café, a world-class music museum, and an inclinator ride to the top. Voted Memphian of the Year in 1989, Shlenker was persona-non-grata by 1991 when, unable to solve his financial problems, he forfeited his contracts and left town. The $63 million stainless-steel Great American Pyramid opened in 1991 with a 22,000 seat arena, but minus the tourist amenities Shlenker had promised. A Ramesses II reproduction stands at the east entrance.

Memphis has a long history of trying to attract and keep major sports teams. The city suffered through a series of ill-fated football teams such as the Memphis Mad Dogs of the Canadian Football League and the Memphis Pharaohs of the Arena Football League. And who could forget the XFL's Memphis Maniax? The Tennessee Oilers of the National Football League stopped off for a few months to play in Memphis until the new stadium in Nashville was ready for them. Memphians showed a noticeable lack of enthusiasm for this temporary franchise.

Baseball fared a little better, but the Double-A Memphis Chicks packed up and left for Jackson in 1997. Storage USA founder Dean Jernigan and his wife, Kristi, tried to purchase them to keep the team in the city. When this failed, they decided to pursue a Triple-A franchise. The Jernigans acquired the St. Louis Cardinals farm team to become the Memphis Redbirds. This franchise would become the first sports team in history to be owned and operated by a not-for-profit foundation; all profits would find their way back into the community to fund youth programs. The Redbirds played in the renovated Tim McCarver Stadium in 1998 and 1999 during construction of the controversial $80 million downtown ball park. Many had argued it should be located in the suburbs, not across the street from the Peabody Hotel at Union and Third. Since its inaugural game on April 1, 2000, AutoZone Park has become a very bright spot in the rejuvenation of downtown Memphis.

The Pyramid, a basketball stadium, was finally the lure for a major league team. The Memphis Rockers of the short-lived World Basketball League came and went. Throughout the late 1970s and early 1980s, it was Memphis State's men's basketball team that inspired the fans. The Tigers enjoyed eight straight winning seasons and eight trips to the NCAA tournament, reaching their peak in 1985 with a Final Four matchup against triumphant Villanova. The city did eventually attract an NBA team, but unfortunately it deemed the Pyramid inadequate. The Vancouver Grizzlies moved into it for their 2001–2002 inaugural season after several million dollars' renovation and the promise of a new arena in downtown by 2004. The new Fed Ex Forum rises from the soil of the old demolished Beale district. The Forum and AutoZone Park bookend the entertainment district of Peabody Place and the revitalized Beale Street in the heart of downtown Memphis.

As the new century began, Memphis leaders turned their attention to the riverfront, devising an ambitious 50-year plan to connect downtown, Mud Island,

and the riverfront into a seamless whole. The core of the plan is a proposal to create 50 acres of new land in the form of a land bridge connecting to Mud Island from Court Street to Poplar Avenue. To the south of the bridge will be a new downtown commercial Harbor at the Cobblestones. Behind it, north of Poplar, will be a newly created lake. The vision is bold and has the potential to complete the renaissance now begun in so many areas of the city.

The revitalization of the built environment in Memphis has also led to a rebirth of the social environment. Voters have elected an array of new political leaders, black and white, to city and county government, many of whom seem committed to a retreat from old animosities and divisions. High tech firms and young professionals are reversing the trend that previously devastated the center city, bringing excitement and vibrant life to downtown. Today's multi-hued Memphis moves into the twenty-first century with a new spirit of cooperation and optimism.

This artist's rendering of the proposed $225 million riverfront development project shows how the land bridge will shape the commercial harbor at the foot of Beale Street and create a recreational lake north of Poplar in front of the Pyramid.

ENDNOTES

1. Carole M. Ornelas-Struve and Frederick Lee Coulter, *Memphis, 1800–1900: Volume I-Years of Challenge*, 1800–1860 (New York: Nancy Powers & Company, Publishers, Incorporated, 1982), 15.
2. Carole Ornelas-Struve, *Memphis, 1800–1900*, 16.
3. James Roper, *The Founding of Memphis, 1818–1820* (Memphis: Memphis Sesquicentennial, Incorporated, 1970), 19.
4. Ibid., 24.
5. Ibid., 30.
6. O.F. Vedders, *History of the City of Memphis and Shelby County*, Tennessee (Syracuse, NY, D. Mason & Co., Publishers, 1888), 17.
7. *Memphis Weekly Eagle*, January 9, 1846.
8. *Memphis Enquirer*, July 22, 1837.
9. Ruthie Ann Maria (Boyd or Bayliss), petition for emancipation, January 1850, Shelby County Quarterly Court, Shelby County Archives (SCA); Ruthie Anna Maria Boyd, Will #1210, Shelby County Probate Court; R. Bayliss or Rutha Bayliss estate, Tax assessment, Memphis Property Tax Assessment Books, 1851 and 1852, SCA.
10. Quoted in John Harkins, *Metropolis of the American Nile* (Oxford Mississippi: The Guild Bindery Press, 1982), 42.
11. Vedders, *History of the City of Memphis and Shelby County*, 18.
12. David Tucker, *Black Pastors & Leaders* (Memphis: Memphis State University Press, 1975), 2.
13 *Memphis Daily Appeal*, 23 August 1851, 11 October 1851, 25 August 1856, 28 December 1856.
14. Vedders, *History of the City of Memphis and Shelby County*, 215.
15. Ibid., 52.
16. Elizabeth Avery Meriwether, *Recollections of 92 years*, 1824–1916 (McLean, Virginia: EPM Publications, Incorporated, 1994), 58.
17. John Keating, *History of Memphis and Shelby County* (Syracuse: D. Mason & Co., 1888), 483.
18. Gerald M. Capers, Jr., *The Biography of A River Town, Memphis: Its Heroic Age* (Gerald M. Capers, Jr., 1966) 155.

19. American Missionary Association, Lucinda Humphrey, 11 June 1863.

20. A.D. Olds to George Whipple, January 9, 1864, AMA.

21. *Memphis Daily Bulletin*, 26 July 1863.

22. *Memphis Daily Bulletin*, 13 and 26 August 1863; Captain Clark, 29 September 1865, Freedmen's Bureau, Rental Agent's report.

23. Davis Tillson correspondence, 15 April 1865, Freedmen's Bureau Records, Rental Agent's report.

24. Lynette Boney Wrenn, *Crisis and Commission Government in Memphis: Elite Rule in a Gilded Age City* (Knoxville: University of Tennessee Press, 1998), 150.

25. Alfreda Duster, *Crusade for Justice: The Autobiography of Ida B. Wells* (Chicago: University of Chicago Press, 1970), 66.

26. Carroll Van West, ed., *Tennessee Encyclopedia of History and Culture* (Nashville: Rutledge Hill Press, 1998), 437.

27. Joan Turner Beifuss, *At the River I Stand* (Memphis: St. Luke's Press, 1990), 147.

28. *Memphis Press-Scimitar*, 1935, quoted by Roger Biles, *Memphis in the Great Depression* (Knoxville: University of Tennessee Press, 1986), 88.

29. Quoted in Helen M. Coppock and Charles W. Crawford, eds., *Paul R. Coppock's Mid-South, Vol. III* (Memphis: Paul R. Coppock Publication Trust, 1993), 119.

30. Carol Lynn Yellin and Janann Sherman, *The Perfect 36: Tennessee Delivers Woman Suffrage* (Oak Ridge, TN: Iris Press, 1998), 68.

31. David Cohn quoted by Robert A. Sigafoos, *Cotton Row to Beale Street: A Business History of Memphis* (Memphis: Memphis State University Press, 1979), 157–58.

32. Emily Yellin, *A History of the Mid-South Fair* (Memphis: Guild Bindery Press, Incorporated, 1995), 21.

33. Biles, *Memphis in the Great Depression*, 24.

34. Ibid., 53.

35. Paul H. Bergeron, et al, *Tennesseans and Their History* (Knoxville: University of Tennessee Press, 1999), 279.

36. Quoted by Peter Guralnick, *Last Train to Memphis: The Rise of Elvis Presley* (Boston: Little, Brown and Company, 1994), 5–6.

37. Quoted in Beifuss, *At the River I Stand*, 172.

38. Quoted by Floyd Montgomery Sharp, *The Desegregation of Memphis City Schools Under the Direction of United States District Judge Robert Malcolm McRae, Jr.* Ph.D. Dissertation, The University of Memphis, 1997), 249–50.

BIBLIOGRAPHY

PRIMARY SOURCES:

All primary sources used in this book came from the files of the Memphis and Shelby County Room of the Memphis-Shelby County Public Library and Information Center, and the Mississippi Valley Collection of the University of Memphis Libraries.

Illustrations came primarily from the Memphis and Shelby County Room of the Memphis-Shelby County Public Library and Information Center, and the Mississippi Valley Collection of the University of Memphis Libraries. Additional illustrations were obtained from the Memphis Redbirds, the Memphis Convention and Visitors' Bureau, Ms. Karen Schaber, the Memphis and Shelby County Airport Authority, the Memphis Riverfront Development Corporation, Looney Ricks Kiss Architects, Incorporated, and the Tennessee State Library and Archives.

SECONDARY SOURCES:

Beifuss, Joan Turner. *At the River I Stand*. Memphis: St. Luke's Press, 1990.

Bergeron, Paul H., Stephen V. Ash and Jeanette Keith. *Tennesseans and Their History*. Knoxville: University of Tennessee Press, 1999.

Biles, Roger. *Memphis in the Great Depression*. Knoxville: University of Tennessee Press, 1986.

Cantor, Louis. *Wheelin' on Beale*. New York: Pharos Books, 1992.

Capers, Gerald. *The Biography of a River Town*. New York: Vanguard, 1966.

Church, Roberta and Ronald Walter; Charles W. Crawford, ed. *Nineteenth Century Memphis Families of Color 1850–1900*. Memphis: Murdock Printing Co., 1987.

Coppock, Helen M. and Charles W. Crawford, eds. *Paul R. Coppock's Mid-South, Vol. I–Vol. IV*. Memphis: Paul R. Coppock Publication Trust, 1985-1994.

Coppock, Paul R. *Memphis Memoirs*. Memphis: Memphis State University Press, 1980.

———. *Memphis Sketches*. Memphis: Friends of Memphis and Shelby County Libraries, 1976.

Crawford, Charles W. *Yesterday's Memphis*. Miami, FL: E.A. Seamann Publishing, Incorporated, 1976.

——— and Terry Keeter, "The Appeal of Memphis: A Retrospective of 15 Decades: April 21, 1841–1991," supplement to *The Commercial Appeal*, 21 April 1991.

Dando, Mary. "Soulsville: How the Dream Will Endure." *Memphis Magazine* Vol. XXVII, No. 4 (2002): 36–39.

Dowdy, G. Wayne. "Censoring Popular Culture: Political and Social Control in Segregated Memphis." *The West Tennessee Historical Society Papers* Vol. LV (2001): 98–117.

Duster, Alfreda, ed. *Crusade for Justice: The Autobiography of Ida B. Wells*. Chicago: University of Chicago Press, 1970.

Fulbright, Jim. *Aviation in Tennessee*. Goodlettsville, TN: Mid-South Publications, 1998.

Gilbert, Debbie, et al. "A Century of Memphis." *Memphis Magazine* Vol. XIX, No. 5 (1994): 8–14, 166–175.

Goings, Kenneth W. and Gerald L. Smith. "Unhidden Transcripts: Memphis and African American Agency, 1862–1920" in Kenneth W. Goings and Raymond A. Mohl, eds. *The New African American Urban History*. Thousand Oaks, CA: Sage Publications, Incorporated, 1996, 146-166.

Guralnick, Peter. *Last Train to Memphis: The Rise of Elvis Presley*. Boston: Little, Brown and Company, 1994.

———. *Sweet Soul Music: Rhythm and Blues and the Southern Dream of Freedom*. Boston: Little, Brown and Company, 1999.

Gordon, Robert. *It Came from Memphis*. Boston: Faber and Faber, 1995.

Hamilton, G.P. *The Bright Side of Memphis*. Memphis: G.P. Hamilton, 1908.

Harkins, John E. *Metropolis of the American Nile*. Memphis: West Tennessee Historical Society, 1982.

Hill, S. Davidson. "The Self-Defined African American Community of Jim Crow Memphis." *West Tennessee Historical Society Papers* Vol. LIV (2000): 1–33.

Keating, John. *History of Memphis and Shelby County*. Syracuse: D. Mason & Company, 1888.

Lauderdale, Vance. *Ask Vance*. Memphis: Bluff City Books, 2003.

Magness, Perre. *Good Abode: Nineteenth Century Architecture in Memphis and Shelby County, Tennessee*. Memphis: The Junior League of Memphis, Incorporated, 1983.

———. *Past Times: Stories of Early Memphis*. Memphis: Parkway Press LLC, 1994.

Marling, Karal Ann. *Graceland*. Cambridge, MA: Harvard University Press, 1996.

Miller, William D. *Memphis During the Progressive Era*. Memphis: Memphis State University Press, 1957.

Morrison, Andrew. *Memphis, Tennessee, The Bluff City: Mistress of the Valley of the Lower River*. St. Louis and Memphis: George W. Engelhardt, 1892.

Pohlmann, Marcus D. and Michael P. Kirby. *Racial Politics at the Crossroads: Memphis Elects Dr. W. W. Herenton*. Knoxville: University of Tennessee Press, 1996.

Raichelson, Richard. *Beale Street Talks*. Memphis: Arcadia Records, 1994.

Roper, James. *The Founding of Memphis, 1818–1820*. Memphis: The Memphis Sesquicentennial, Incorporated, 1970.

Sharp, Floyd Montgomery. *The Desegregation of Memphis City Schools Under the Direction of United States District Judge Robert Malcolm McRae, Jr.* Ph.D. Dissertation, The University of Memphis, 1997.

Shelby County's Shame: The Story of the Big Creek Lynching Trial. Memphis, 1895.

Sigafoos, Robert A. *Cotton Row to Beale Street: A Business History of Memphis*. Memphis: Memphis State University Press, 1979.

Tucker, David M. *Lieutenant Lee of Beale Street*. Nashville: Vanderbilt University Press, 1971.
———. *Black Pastors and Leaders: Memphis, 1819–1972*. Memphis: Memphis State University Press, 1975.

———. *Memphis Since Crump: Bossism, Blacks and Civic Reformers, 1948–1968*. Knoxville: University of Tennessee Press, 1979.

Van West, Carroll, ed. *Tennessee Encyclopedia of History and Culture*. Nashville: Rutledge Hill Press, 1998.

Vedders, O.F. *History of the City of Memphis and Shelby County, Tennessee*. Syracuse, NY: D. Mason & Co., Publishers, 1888.

Walk, Joe. *A History of African-Americans in Memphis Government*. Joe Walk, 1996.

Wedell, Marsha. *Elite Women and the Reform Impulse in Memphis, 1875–1915*. Knoxville: University of Tennessee Press, 1991.

Worley, William S. *Beale Street: Crossroads of America's Music*. Lenexa, KS: Addax Publishing Group, 1998.

Wrenn, Lynette Boney. *Crisis and Commission Government in Memphis*. Knoxville: University of Tennessee Press, 1998.

Yellin, Carol Lynn and Janann Sherman. *The Perfect 36: Tennessee Delivers Woman Suffrage*. Oak Ridge, TN: Iris Press, 1998.

Yellin, Emily. *A History of the Mid-South Fair*. Memphis: Guild Bindery Press, Incorporated, 1995.

INDEX

www.ingramcontent.com/pod-product-compliance
Lightning Source LLC
Chambersburg PA
CBHW050616110426
42813CB00008B/2579